A HISTORY OF THE NIKYOB (KANINKON) PEOPLE, FROM EARLIEST TIMES TO 2000

A HISTORY OF THE NIKYOB (KANINKON) PEOPLE, FROM EARLIEST TIMES TO 2000

Godwin Danjuma Kwalbe

GALDA VERLAG 2025

Bibliografische Information der Deutschen Nationalbibliothek
Die Deutsche Nationalbibliothek verzeichnet diese Publikation in der Deutschen
Nationalbibliografie; detaillierte bibliografische Daten sind im Internet über
https://dnb.de abrufbar.

ISBN 978-3-96203-444-3 (Print)
ISBN 978-3-96203-445-0 (E-Book)

TABLE OF CONTENTS

DEDICATION   i

FOREWORD   iii

ACKNOWLEDGEMENTS   v

PREFACE   vii

Section One:
Pre-Colonial Period

Introduction   3

Chapter One: Land and Environment   5

Location   5

Topography   5

Climate   6

Hydrology and Water Resources   6

Flora and Fauna   6

Human and Mineral Resources   7

Chapter Two: History and Socio-Political Organization   9

Origins and Migration   9

Extinct Clans   15

Socio-Political Set-up   16

Religious Worldview   18

Cultural Practices and Initiation Rites   21

Changing Demographics in the 19th Century   24

Economic Activities   25

Arts and Entertainment   27

Inter-Group Relations   27

Nikyob History and Jama'a Emirate   29

Dangoma in Nikyob History   35

Section Two:
Colonial Period

Chapter Three: Colonial Conquest   39

British Colonial Conquest of Nikyob Land and Resistance   39

The Indirect Rule System   45

Christian Missionary Activities   46

Section Three:
Post-Colonial Period

Chapter Four: Asserting Self-Identity within Independent Nigeria   51

Chapter Five: The Place of Kafanchan in Nikyob (Kaninkon) History   53

History of Kafanchan Town and its many Dimensions   53

The Growth and Development of Kafanchan Town   55

Kafanchan: A Place or an Ethnic Group?   62

Kafanchan in Nikyob History   63

Chapter Six: Conclusion   69

BIBLIOGRAPHY   71

ABOUT THE AUTHOR   79

DEDICATION

This book is heartily dedicated to the loving memory of my parents:
Mr. Danjuma Gaga Kwalbe and Mrs. Yelwa Danjuma Kwalbe

&

My sisters:
Patience Danjuma Kwalbe and Antonia Danjuma Kwalbe.

FOREWORD

This book – *A History of the Nikyob (Kaninkon) People* is very important as it will be to the best of my knowledge, the first formally documented History of the Nikyob (Kaninkon) people. The lateness of this publication is not deliberate but is a reflection of the late literacy development of the people. A book cannot be written without some form of literacy which is the ability to read and write and being able to read and write is possible only through learning. In this part of the country, Southern Kaduna (formerly Southern Zaria), literacy was introduced by the missionaries whose activities are said to have formally started in Ham land – Kwoi to be exact in 1910. This privilege reached Kaninkon land in the 1930s as a result of the coming of the Sudan Interior Mission (S.I.M.) to Kagoro in 1927 – led by Rev. Archibald (popularly and locally known as Dacip) which then reached Kafanchan and Kaninkon in the early 1930s. The first literate man in Nikyob was the late Pastor Tete Burat (1905 – 1963) who became a Christian in 1932 as well as the first Pastor in the land around 1937 after training in Kagoro Bible School.

Before now, the history of the Nikyob people has been orally transmitted- and we know how short human memory can be. Apart from human short memory, there is a tendency of lack of objectivity in such oral history. The most objective source of history in an area such as Southern Kaduna is the reports and records of the European administrators – District Officers and Residents, and the Provincial Officers. It is good that some of their reports are still found in archives and old records. Their reports are more accurate and more reliable – even though their understanding of the history of the people and their environment was limited. The cultures of the people and the areas would appear to have been confusing to them – differentiation of say Nikyob (they called them Kaninkwom), Kaje (now Bajju), Kagoro, Gwong (Kagoma) was not easy to the European administrators.

It is good that this book covers areas like the topography, climate of the area, natural resources, and the occupation of the people from time immemorial. All these affect people's way of life. It is from this point of view that traditional practices like – initiation, dos and don'ts of the people are covered. The initiations were in stages – from the ages of about 14 and 15 up to about 20 years of age. Only about one or in rare cases two initiations were done after marriage. The initiation rites made a person (male only) properly become "a man" who could face life with confidence.

Colonial rule and the coming of the Missionaries were very significant and literarily changed the entire traditional set-up. The construction of the railway which was mainly to convey agricultural and mineral resources was a game changer. It was mainly the purpose of conveying tin and columbite from Jos and the surrounding areas that the railway was constructed to Jos and eventually to Bauchi and beyond. Kafanchan, formerly just a village became not only a station but a junction to both Jos and Kaduna. A town developed initially pushing the indigenes to the hinterland but eventually became a center of both commerce and governance. The headquarters of the emirate – Jama'a Emirate – was moved from Jama'a Sarari (Madakiya) to Kafanchan and the town became a well-planned town – a "strangers' town" as the indigenes were sadly, not part of the town. Even the emirate only came in around 1933-4 from old-Jama'a. Since it became a metropolis, Kafanchan town has been growing rather slowly when compared to other places like Minna, Makurdi, Jos and other towns due to many reasons that are the subject of another book.

It can be seen that the coming of colonial rule as well as the arrival of the missionaries resulted in the growth of Kafanchan into a metropolis. This has not only been very significant in the growth of the Nikyob (Kaninkon) but also its neighbors and the entire area. The changes brought about affected the way of life of the people – culturally, economically, and their world view. It is hoped that people will find this book interesting and hopefully more research and books will be published as a result of this historical account of Nikyob.

HRH Tanko Tete
Kafanchan
August, 2023

ACKNOWLEDGEMENTS

My life is completely the product of grace; the glory for everything that I am today is ascribed unto the LORD who has made me a reference point. I did not have what it takes to accomplish anything in destiny, from my early years. But today I am what I am because of Him. A work like this cannot be done without assistance from people. Therefore, I am indebted to mention a few due to the constraints of space and time.

I am eternally grateful to God for my wife Grace; she is a gift to my life and not just a spouse. Some things have been possible because she has provided the enabling environment and her tolerance of some of my excess ideological baggage picked from the radical Zaria School of Historical Thought. I equally appreciate the children Teb-Rik, Veh-Tum, and Nnyok-Rik, I am always eager to come home after every day's taxing schedules because your hugs at the door have always been refreshing and reassuring. Without all of you, life would be boring. May God also bless my siblings, Jidi, Grace, and Gladys for their invaluable contribution to my life.

My eternal gratitude goes to my parents who believed in me and practically sacrificed their lives for me to be where I am today. To be sincere, aside from God, my parents were my lifetime support and heroes. I am also highly indebted to my spiritual parents Apostle and Pastor Mrs. Emmanuel Egoh Bako for their mentoring roles and trust. The entire pastoral team of Good News Power Base Church, 17 Abuja Street, Kafanchan, where my whole life has revolved since graduating from the university is appreciated. All members of the ministry that I cannot be able to mention by name, their contributions to the success story of my life, are highly appreciated.

Exceptional gratitude is due to His Royal Highness Tanko Tete for his fatherly encouragement and motivation in the course of this research. His love for knowledge and the progress of Nikyob Land is second to none. Throughout my years of research, I have found the duo of The Reverend Barr. Wakili Kadima, and Architect Ishaku Bakau very helpful. They have graciously released their rich collections to me and have given me valuable insights into the issues around this research, mostly during discussion sessions. I take sole responsibility for any weakness in this book but share the credit with both of them.

My colleagues at the Department of History Kaduna, State University, whom I have enjoyed the best of moments, sometimes as colleagues and other times as mentors, have been significant in my career growth within the academia. I cannot but mention them by names: Professor Abdullahi M. Ashafa, Professor T. Wuam, Professor G. Jatau, Dr. N. Abubakar, Dr. A. Sani, Dr. S. Shehu, Dr. A. Tor, Dr. I. Danmaraya, Dr. A. Ibrahim, Dr. M. Buhari, Mr. J. Danjuma, Ms. H. Musa, Mr. H. Aboi, Mr. S. Yohanna, Mr. M. Adamu, and Mr. S. Richifa.

I am particularly grateful to my mother Dr. Hannatu Kwasau who read and edited the work. She gave me positive comments that further boosted my confidence. I pray for you to be strengthened and preserved by the Lord.

To everyone I have ever shared any close moment in life with; you share in my success story and cannot be ignored in a moment like this. However, because it is impossible to list all people in a section of acknowledgments, your names are written on the tablet of my heart. May you receive your reward from the Lord of the universe!

PREFACE

This book is a culmination of many years of my desire to know more about myself and the socio-cultural constituency I belong to. Having a bachelor's degree in history and my undergraduate project work was on the evolution and development of Kafanchan Town, it, therefore, means that I had to go to places like the National Archives, Kaduna and Arewa House, Kaduna. The implication is that I stumbled on one or two documents that further spurred my interest in the issues around this area. Additionally, my research also meant that I needed to conduct interviews. While doing this, I realized that I needed to dig further because I was fed with half-truths, myths, and assumptions. I have planned to obtain my Ph.D. first before venturing into the reconstruction of the history of the Nikyob People but circumstances made me to change my plan and here we have the first book on Nikyob history.

Additionally, from that period to date, much has happened that has helped to disorganize that principle making me shift grounds. Of significance is the Professor Kenetth Dike Memorial Lecture delivered by Professor C.B.N. Ogbogbo at Hotel Sylvia, No. 66 Ezillo Avenue, Independence Layout Enugu, Enugu State, during the 66th Conference/Congress of the Historical Society of Nigeria (HSN), 2021. The guest lecturer particularly struck me as a person when he said "If historians do not write the history of their areas, nonprofessionals will write a distorted version of it and it will become widespread."

Likewise, His Royal Highness Mr. Tanko Tete gave me an assignment to write an abridged version of the Nikyob History as content for the council's website being built. It was this responsibility by the paramount ruler that became the greatest motivation for this book. There were no books for me to consult to bring this assignment to fruition. In order words, I was to start everything from scratch. Premised on this realization, I decided to embark on a complete work, complete in the sense of a book, but not as a finality of the research into the history of Nikyob People.

Essentially, the thrust of this research is to write the history of Nikyob with a professional touch against the many legends and assumptions about a people whose contribution to the development of the entire area right from pre-colonial days into the modern era is oblivious.

Ultimately, the available internal evidence of this region disagrees with most of the stories of origins and migrations from places like Kano, Bauchi, Taraba, and the most popular, Katsina-Ala. If anything, these may only signal some kinds of socio-economic, cultural, and diplomatic transactions that have helped to strengthen bilateral ties across geographical enclaves. In the end, the conclusion is consistent with other seminal and groundbreaking research in the entire Southern Kaduna and Central Nigerian area to the extent that this current work is an extension of other bodies of research by scholars of repute. Consequently, I am happy to be the one who has set the stage for other follow-up research about the Nikyob People.

Godwin Danjuma Kwalbe
Kaduna
August, 2023

SECTION ONE: PRE-COLONIAL PERIOD

INTRODUCTION

This book explores the rich history of the Nikyob people that has largely remained undocumented except for some parchments here and there and also oral accounts that have hitherto not been corroborated. It is accepted in the field of historical studies that reconstructing the history of any society can never be a one-off exercise but a continuous process of reinterpretation and reorganization of data in the face of discoveries. Therefore, this work is not the end but the beginning of series of Nikyob history. Having made this point, it is also very important to state that this project is very significant to the Nikyob nation because it will remain a solid foundation for future historians to build on. What this means is that the reader is currently interacting with groundbreaking material in terms of a deliberate and professional reconstruction of our history. The reason for this is that man is both a product and/or a continuum of the past, hence the need to not only know it but appreciate it for a better society.

In order to answer the myriad of questions before us, the research methodology that was adopted is the use of primary and secondary sources. This agrees with the standard practice as far as reconstructing Nigerian and African history is concerned. What this portends is that for a non-literate society like ours, reconstructing its history cannot be possible without delving into oral sources that have been retrieved through interviews with members of the society who have been privileged to know some of the information transferred from one generation to another. More so, very vital components of data within the primary sources are the archival documents. This is firsthand information kept at the National Archives, Kaduna; made up of written minutes, memorandums, quarterly and yearly reports; and all forms of correspondence by colonial officials during the period of British Colonial rule. Their import in reconstructing Nikyob history is enormous and therefore cannot be overemphasized. This is also taken in conjunction with unpublished manuscripts by individuals and several memorandums by Community Development Associations. On the other hand, the secondary sources are those data in the form of published works most of which did not set out to reconstruct a complete history of Nikyob but provided us with some insights. These are either works by European or Nigerian writers.

Consequently, it is the ability to rigorously scrutinize these available sources that the reader now has this piece which as stated earlier, is not final but is doubtlessly reliable. The book has been divided into three sections. Section one is basically on the pre-colonial period of our history which begins with a geographical survey of the land and environment to show what attracted our forefathers to settle here and not elsewhere. This is followed by the second chapter which investigates the history and basic social and political life of Nikyob society before the contact with colonial agents and Christian Missionaries which brought a lot of discontinuity and transformation.

Logically, the next unit that follows is section two which focused on the colonial period. This is a demonstration of the extent to which colonialism and Christianity impacted the Nikyob society and the ability of the people to survive the sudden infiltration of their culture and society. It showed also, what has changed and what has continued during and after colonialism.

The last section is an assessment of the post-colonial era and how Nikyob people have responded to the inevitable change that the entire African continent has gone through. The essence of this particular study is to show the ability of a person to adjust and not remain static while others are making significant progress. This unit also includes an unbiased study of the history of Kafanchan as a village and later as a cosmopolitan town that emerged in the second decade of the 20th Century; and not an ethnic group as it has metamorphosed into as a result of urbanization. The work concludes with a highlight of major discoveries and their contributions to modern scholarship.

CHAPTER ONE:
LAND AND ENVIRONMENT

i. Location

Geographically, Nikyob land is located within longitude 8^0 21' E and latitude 9^0 29' 31' N.[1] In recent times; it is bounded to the north by Jama'a Emirate and to the north-west by Bajju Chiefdom. To the east, it shares a boundary with Fantswam and Kagoro Chiefdoms, and then it is bounded by Godogo Chiefdom in the south.[2] In the early 20th Century, according to the Anthropological Map of Plateau Province, Nikyob had the following ethnic groups as neighbors: Kagoro, Ningom, Numana, Ninzam, Yeskwa, Kagoma, and Kaje.[3]

ii. Topography

The community is characterized by a low-lying topography that drops gently westward from the Kagoro Hills which form part of the Jos Plateau. The general slope of the land extends from the Plateau to the Kagoma Scarp and the Kwoi-Nok and Chori Plateau which again punctuates this undulating country side that becomes very rugged. Consequently, several valleys and deep gulleys are created by this type of relief system; they are mostly natural. Generally speaking, the geology of Nikyob Land is a basement complex consisting of pre-Cambrian igneous rocks-the resultant effect of weathering which has given rise to the red tropical lateritic soils that become very muddy and sticky in the rainy season and dusty in the dry season.[4]

---

[1] M. Moses, "Levels and Differentials in Fertility at Kafanchan", (M.A. Geography, A.B.U. Zaria, 1985), p. 48.

[2] Tanko Tete, *A Life of Service: An Autobiography of Sarkin Kaninkon (Tum Nikyob),* (Makurdi: Aboki Publishers, 2020), p. 14.

[3] J.C. Sciortino, *The Gazetteer of Nasarawa Province, (London*: Frank Cass & Co. Ltd., *1920),* p. 5.

[4] S. Sankey, "An Economic Geographical Survey of Kafanchan-Kaduna State", (B.A. Geography, A.B.U. Zaria, 1983), pp. 5-6.

iii.   Climate

Because of its location on the windward side of the Kagoro Hills which forms the southern escarpment of the Jos Plateau, the prevailing trade winds are the south-west and north-east trade winds. The former is responsible for the rains (orographic type) averaging about 150cm-200cm (1500mm-2000mm) from April to October. The north-east trade wind is dry, dusty, and cold, experienced between November to March. All these are responsible for the wet and dry seasons with an annual mean temperature of about 78^0f , typical of Savanna areas.[5]

iv.   Hydrology and Water Resources

The general height of the community is between 2,400 and 2,420ft. above sea level. To the west is river Matsirga popularly referred to as River Wonderful with its fairly broad plains. This river meanders into Nikyob Land and along with other streams, provides several sources of water for domestic works, dry season farming, and rearing of livestock. This has made available varieties of aquatic animals and sea food. There are in addition to these animals, along the banks of the rivers, trees of utmost economic importance for the existence of human life such as palm trees and bamboo trees. All are useful for economic activities. By and large, the marshlands that result from the action of over flooding are relatively fertile for agriculture which is the mainstay of the people.[6]

v.   Flora and Fauna

Having the advantage of being situated within the northern Guinea Savanna, the land forms a transition zone between the forest and the savanna belts. It comprises transitional woodland as its climax vegetation. This supports the existence of valuable economic trees like shea butter, tamarind, locust beans, iroko tree, silk cotton, ebony tree, fig tree, delep palm, rubber climber, mahogany, mango, etc. This area had long served as a viable hunting ground for the Nikyob people with several big games such as buffalos, roan antelopes, leopard, porcupine, apes, a few lions, etc. However, due to heavy and increasing

---

[5]   S. Sankey, "An Economic Geographical Survey", pp. 5-6.
[6]   S. Sankey, "An Economic Survey", pp. 5-6.

human activities such as agriculture, bush burning, deforestation, and mining over the years, the vegetation has significantly changed into scattered tall trees and grasses. The plains are highly suitable for grazing and cultivation of a wide variety of food and cash crops.[7]

vi.   Human and Mineral Resources

The whole of Nikyob land is blessed with countless resources. Whether under the soil, water, or on the land surface, one would be engaged in a great battle gathering the list of all the resources. In terms of its human population, the demography is composed of highly fearless, resilient, intelligent, and foresighted individuals. Both women and men are known for the ability to undertake great and difficult tasks; this is a blessing often ignored by some when discussing the wealth of a society. In terms of mineral resources, there are precious metals of high quality in large commercial quantities that include: tin-ore, nickel, tantalite, columbite, mica (muscovite), beryl (aquamarine), emerald, tourmaline, corundum (sapphire), royal blue, topaz, garnet, amethyst, etc.[8] These are just some of the few mineral deposits in the Nikyob land area. It is believed that there are many more waiting to be discovered.

---

[7]   Ibrahim James, *Studies in the History, Politics and Cultures of Southern Kaduna Peoples Groups*, (Jos, Ladsomas Press Limited, 1997), p.1, Tanko Tete, *A Life of Service*, p. 14.

[8]   Kaduna Mining Development Co. LTD. (KDMC), "Mineral Endowments" https://kmdc.kdsg.gov.ng/mineral-endowments/ (31-08-2022).

CHAPTER TWO:

HISTORY AND SOCIO-POLITICAL ORGANISATION

i. Origin and Migration

In this book, I have chosen to consistently use **Nikyob** against **Kaninkon** to refer to this people. There is absolutely nothing wrong with either of them; what matters is maintaining the same pattern from beginning to end. Both have their place in history. The former is the native name and simply means *Ni* (descendants) of *Kyob* while the latter became popular during the slave raiding days perpetrated by the Hausa people. It is a term that came from the Nikyob people during some of these life-and-death struggles. Progressively, it became a name used by the Hausa to refer to this group, since they did not understand what they were saying or what name they bore, they decided to call them Kaninkon. The term came from *kan (come) ti (let us) kom (*war).[9] It was a call for war among them in the face of the advancing enemies. Within the field of historical studies, it is accepted that one should refer to a group by the name it was called in the period being reconstructed and documented in the available literature. However, since this study went back beyond the period of written records, it is safe to maintain the group's name and not the imposed one.

Additionally, it is important to note that the name Nikyob refers to the people and not the language. The language is called *Myod*. In deeper inter-personal transactions among members of Nkyob society, *myod* is used as a demand for an individual to say and live out the truth, nothing more, and nothing less. This goes to shed light on the value placed on integrity/sincerity by society. Any untoward attitude was regarded as strange and considered not part of the nature of the Nikyob people.

---

[9]   Bauta D. Motty, *Indigenous Christian Discipleship-Makig,* (Jos, ECWA Productions Ltd. 2013), pp. 22-23.

As has been stated in the introduction, the Nikyob people are part of the non-literate societies (in pre-colonial times); this means that they could not document their history. Therefore, the bulk of what is known about their origin and migration comes from oral accounts and few written documents in the late 19th and beginning of the 20th Centuries mostly by colonial writers. With the introduction of western education, some people have been able to document their information in the form of manuscripts which are also reservoirs of historical data useful for historical reconstruction.

The popular tradition within the society has it that the people originated from Benue State at Katsina-Ala. Some of the proponents of this tradition hold the opinion that the ancestors of the Nikyob people left Katsina-Ala for the new sites in search of new farmlands and hunting grounds[10]. Another legend traces the origin to an unspecified place in the present-day Bauchi State.[11] It should be noted, however, that these and many others are still at the level of mere claims and legends that would be properly interpreted below. The central lesson from these accounts is the fact that migration is as long as the existence of human beings on earth, especially on the African continent believed to be the home of early man. This is based on the diversity of DNA and multiple ethnic groups.[12] Instructively, one of Nigeria's foremost historians in the person of Obaro Ikime has consistently argued in his writings, most of these traditions of origins were usually formulated to gain some status of superiority before new neighbors and/or to claim a connection to places of political power/authority. In essence, they are not to be taken as historical truths.[13]

Therefore, in the case of Nikyob, the only valid historical truth in the above legends of migration is to tell us that there had been movement from one location to another within the area of study. These movements were usually in search of new and fertile farmlands, viable hunting grounds; and relocating away from epidemic-prone areas, wild beasts, and also in the past, slave raiders and colonial exploitative tax system. Other than this, the Nikyob people have long lived in their present location. This position is more

---

[10]   Bauta D. Motty, *Indigenous Christian Discipleship-Making*, p. 6.

[11]   Bauta D. Motty, *Indigenous Christian*, p.6; Kaninkon Chiefdom, *The Pioneers*. (n.d.), Hill-Side Production, p.1; Tanko Tete. *A Life of Service*, p. 16.

[12]   Roscoe Stanyon, Marco Sazzini & Donata Luiselli, "Timing the First Migration into Eastern Asia" in *Journal of Biology, ISSN: 1475-4924*, 2009. Accessed at https://doi.org/10.1186/jbiol115 (22/08/2022).

[13]   See, Obaro Ikime. *History, The Historian and The Nation: The Voice of a Nigerian Historian.* (Ibadan, Heinemann Educational Books (Nigeria) PLC, 2006).

authoritative when pieces of evidence from archaeology and linguistics are interrogated.

In carrying out a historical survey of the Southern Kaduna Zone, Simon Yohanna came up with this conclusion:

> "These groups are so interrelated linguistically, culturally and economically that we have no option than to concede that they come from same parent body. The differences in these groups of dialects may indicate a stream of migration…"[14]

The implication of this revelation to understanding the history of Nikyob and debunking the myth of our ancestors coming from Benue, Kano, Katsina, Taraba, or Bauchi States is that their current neighbors share a lot in common with them in terms of socio-cultural setup and linguistic affinities than with other groups far away. In line with the language family, these various linguistic groups have been classified as Benue-Congo or Semi-Bantu groups.[15] This is because their language structures are similar.[16] This similarity may not be a general and visible rule, especially in terms of intelligibility but can be deduced through sub-group studies. For instance, according to Simon Yohanna, the Kaje, Kataf, Moro'a, Attakar, Kagoro, and Kafanchan form a language cluster while the Ikulu, Kuturmi, and Kadara form another. Then the Jaba, Koro, and Kamantan form a language cluster.[17] Interestingly, Nikyob belongs to another linguistic cluster that are mutually intelligibility; these are Mada, Numana, Ninzo, Gwandara, Kanufi, etc.[18] However, it must be noted that the unique nature of the Nikyob language does not neatly fit into this classification above (Semi-Bantu) in terms of similarities with the listed groups. It is different but similar to other languages like the "Ayu, Gwandara…Kibo, Ningwom and Numana".[19]

What this foregoing argument means to understand our subject is that most ethnic groups within this area are mutually intelligible, especially those nearby. This strengthens the position that our existence in this area has been for a very long time because our immediate neighbors as outlined in the third cluster are those that we share similar features with culturally and

---

[14]   Simon Yohanna, "Southern Zaria", p. 10.
[15]   Yusuf Turaki, *The British Colonial Legacy*, p. 27.
[16]   Yusufu Turaki, *The British Colonial Legacy*, p. 27.
[17]   Simon Yohanna, "Southern Zaria", p. 10.
[18]   Tanko Tete, *A life of Service*, pp. 16-17.
[19]   NAK: PLA PROF "Provincial Gazetteer", 29th January, 1932.

linguistically. Moreover, convincing evidence from archaeology supports the ongoing debate that Nikyob people have been around for a long time in their present location. This strong substantiation is provided by the ancient Nok Civilization.

In the year 1944, an exceptionally fine head of terracotta was found 25ft deep during tin mining close to Kafanchan; after careful analyses by scholars, it was concluded that its presence is a confirmation that human life has been in existence in this area for many centuries back. This is true as carbon dating revealed that the work of art was from a period between 900 BC - 200 AD.[20] Also, scholars hold firmly to the conclusion that those who created the Nok Civilisation are direct ancestors of the present inhabitants. This conclusion is arrived at due to striking similarities in the features found on several artifacts such as the hairstyle, tribal marks, and also the agricultural farm tools still being used by present-day inhabitants. Here is an authoritative finding to this position:

> "The Nok people appear likely to have been the ancestors of the present population of this part of Nigeria and appear to have enjoyed an economy and way of life nearly, if not quite as advanced as that of the present inhabitants".[21]

It is now important to state here that the reader should be aware that the name 'Nok' given to this civilization is generic. It should not be mistaken to mean an innovation that is specific to the Jaba or Ham people of Nok as many erroneously believe. But it is used as an identity for a civilization that spanned across the entire Southern Kaduna and most of Central Nigeria.

Furthermore, Kazah-Toure also believes strongly that most of the groups in the Southern Kaduna area are autochthonous with not much origin or contact with the outside world. This has made them culturally and linguistically unique and exclusive in comparison with many Nigerian groups.[22] Yusufu Turaki again in his seminal work also concludes that:

---

[20] B.E.B. Fagg, "The Nok Culture in Pre-History", in *Journal of Historical Society of Nigeria, Vol.1, No.1.* Ibadan, University Press, 1957, pp. 288-293.

[21] B.E.B. Fagg, "The Nok Culture in Pre-History", p. 288.

[22] Toure Kazah-Toure, "The Political Economy of Ethnic Conflicts and Governance in Southern Kaduna, Nigeria: [De] Constructing a Contested Terrain" in *Africa Development, Vol.24, No.1/2, ISSN. 08503907,* 1999, pp. 109-144. accessed at https://www.Jstor.org/stable/24484540 on 16/08/2022, p. 112.

> "The Gong, Ham (Jaba), Ninkyop, Rindem and Nyankpa
> have no history of migration. These ethnic groups have an
> ancient history of having originated from one place near
> Fadan Kagoma".[23]

All this evidence adds up to one truth; which is that the Nikyob have long
lived in their present location. There also exist reports and mentions made
of Nikyob people within this area as far back as 1810 in written records.[24]
The man by the name Roro who hosted Mallam Usman of Kebbi at the foot
of the Kagoro Mountains was a Nikyob man with his descendants now at
the present Nindem community. This has been further corroborated by the
anthropological report in which the origin of the Nikyob people is described
as unknown.[25] This declaration implies that this writer could not trace the
people anywhere beyond their present site. A few years into the establishment
of British colonial rule in the area, references have been made by its agents to
the existence of various Nikyob communities. For example, on 14 June 1905, a
report by the Assistant Resident of Jema'a mentioned people and communities
within the area of study in which Nikyob as an ethnic group is shown to be
occupying the present location:

> "On my return from Chunje I sent out again through Kafan
> chan, but got no answer. I then sent through Kafanchan
> and I was told that if I camped at Kafan chan all the Kagoro
> would come in, but that they feared to come to Jema'a".[26]

The Chunje being referred to in the above report is Tsonje in Kagoro
which furnishes the reader with more information about the entire landscape
thereby confirming that when the Europeans arrived, our parents were already
on the ground. Another report in 1915 by the Acting Resident of Nasarawa
Province J.C. Sciortino provides additional information in line with the
foregoing argument: "Early in the quarter two Jemaa boys were sent by their
father to collect ashes at Kaninkwom."[27] There is huge historical relevance in
this short sentence which is that, in 1915, Jemaa was still at Jama'a-Da-Roro
(Jama'a-Na-Roro), the present Gidan Waya. For the boys to have been sent by

---

[23] Yusufu Turaki, *The British Colonial Legacy*, p. 26.
[24] A.H.M. Kirk-Greene, *Gazetteers of Northern Provinces of Nigeria, Vol.III; The Central Kingdom*, (London: Frank Cass and Co. Ltd., 1972), p. 13.
[25] J.C. Sciortino, *The Gazetter of Nasarawa Province*, (London: Frank Cass & Co. Ltd., *1920*), p. 5.
[26] NAK: SNP 3763/1911 "Nasarawa Province; Report for June Quarter, 1911", p. 16.
[27] NAK: NAS PROF 94P/1915 "Second Quarterly Report 1914".

their father to collect ashes at Kaninkwom is a clear evidence that the Nikyob people were spread around the Fulanis who were then few in number. Also, the existence of Nikyob communities at Gidan Waya and environs today is a continuation and not a recent innovation. Again, another report in the same year gives the name of one of the villages:

> "The serikin Kaninkwom Amban has been in. He reports that in the attack on the Sergeant Major at Amban quarter of Kaninkwom eight were killed and two wounded. Among the former are included the Madaiki and the Galadima".[28]

This report is another piece of evidence to dispute postulations suggesting that the Nikyob people are later comers in their present land. It is now very clear and undisputable that they have long dwelt in the present site since time immemorial.

Having given this background information, it is important to now state that the Nikyob people are autochthonous to the area of Jema'a Local Government. The society is made up of three integral units - Mbechio, Turan, and Nindem.[29] Today, with all the historical, cultural, and linguistic affinities, Nindem would prefer to be regarded as a separate and distinct ethnic group.[30] Consequently, two groups with six family units in total are now prominent; Turan with the following family units: Kper (Amere), Kyung (Bakin-Kogi), Ngahtiyem (Gerti), and Gbehtiyo made up of Gharas (Ungwan Fari), Ngahkyob (Ungwan Baki) and Kpankon (Amban). The reality of these two major sub-divisions of the Nikyob people (Mbechio and Turan) is essentially family lines. They also make the two ruling houses in the current dispensation.[31]

The ancestor of Nikyob is said to have given birth to two male children - Turan and Gbehtiyo. Turan married two wives one of whom gave birth to three children; Kyung and Ngahtiyem were children of the same mother while Kper alone came from the second wife of Turan. Then Gbetiyo also had two wives from whom one gave birth to two children - Ngahkyob and Gharas. The other wife was the mother of Kpahkon.[32] From these family units, the Nikyob people have grown into what it is today. This is besides the lost groups who

---

28   NAK: NAS PROF 984/1915 " 'G' COMPANY, ON MADA PATROL", by J.C. Sciortino.

29   Bauta D. Motty, *Indigenous Christian Disciple-Making*, p. 7.

30   See, Hussaini Adamu Abdul, "Pre-Colonial History of Nindem and Their Neighbours in Godogodo Chiefdom, Kaduna State, Up To 1904", (Unpublished M.A. Project Submitted to Department of History, Kaduna State University, 2018).

31   Kaninkon Chiefdom, *The Pioneers*, (n.d.), Hill-Side Production, p.9.

32   Tanko Tete, *A Life of Service*, p. 22.

got integrated into other ethnic groups like the Kagoro and Kagoma because of wonderful inter-group cooperation[33] and some are said to have become extinct as stated below.

For marriage convenience, the various families are divided into clans. Kyung consists of three main clans namely; Kimizyok, Kigyem, and Yajot. Kigyem was later divided into four clans such as Biyobyom, Myenmok, Digem, and Songah.[34] Gharas has Na-Be and Ni-Jahr; while Ngahkyob has the following clans: Ni-Batuk, Na-Gweh, Ni-Damsak, Ni-Gbonkok, and Ni-Gyum. The clans in Kper are Machong, Bagu, Myehmok and Nbwengrhaing.

ii. Extinct Clans

Historically, Nikyob had many groups; some got assimilated into other ethnic groups due to proximity and good intergroup relations while some are said to have been completely lost. The account of the latter unit may be unconfirmed and sounds more legendary than historical; however, what is generally important while studying this aspect is the understanding that Nikyob people once occupied an area beyond what it is known today. It is common place in oral accounts to hear of Nikyob family units living in places outside Jema'a Local Government and even the shores of Kaduna State.

Nabol

They are said to be exceptionally skillful so much so that they could bore holes through *acca* (hungry rice) seeds and pass strings through them used in adornment. Their women were also acclaimed to have ignited fire from their fingers whenever they needed to cook. At a particular time when a planned attack against them was leaked, they responded by organizing a celebration in the open. The enemies approached them intending to annihilate but the ground under them opened and immediately they all went down. Their attackers advanced to the spot but did not see anyone but heard the sounds of drums, songs, and dances underground. Their response was to abandon the idea of pursuing them.

---

[33] Tanko Tete, *A Life of Service*, pp. 15-16.
[34] Tanko Tete, A Life of Service, p. 9.

Nakoh

This community was defeated during the war between them and Nitulan. The defeat led to their withdrawal from Nikyob Land. They ascribed this misfortune to one of their women who prepared a delicacy *sun su* from *acca* and left it on a log of wood.

Nigbom

Another legendary family unit was Nigbom; a people who lived without anyone dying among them until they became envious of their neighbors who usually bath their deaths, mourn, and bury them. Nigbom started imitating this practice using logs of wood and later, killing monkeys to prepare for burial. The consequence of this mimicking burial ceremony was that their land became ravaged by death and all except one was spared.[35]

Placing these accounts into proper historical perspective, the reader can deduce the fact that there is a Nikyob population beyond what is known today. It also reveals the high level of civilization built by their ancestors to survive in their environment and compete favorably with their neighbors. There also existed fierce inter and intragroup conflicts that led to loss of lives and/or separation.

iii.   Socio-Political Set-up

On the socio-political set up of the Nikyob people, a colonial officer, A.B. Matthews states thus:

> Kaninkon originally had one chief for the whole tribe and separate priests for each village. During Fulani times the two sections: the Black Kaninkon and White Kaninkon fell out with one another because the latter who are regarded as being of lower status than the black Kaninkon, refused any longer as a reservoir for providing their fair share of the annual tribute of slaves to Jamaa. So they seceded and made

---

[35] Jacob Jatau, "Taka itace Tahirin Kaninkon", Unpublished Manuscript, (n.d.); Ayuba Adon, "Kaningkon and Their Neighbours", Unpublished manuscript, (n.d.).

their own chief and their own arrangements about tribute to Jamaa.[36]

At a glance, the above report presents a picture, especially to non-professional historians that the Nikyob people had a centralized political system. One must note that most of these colonial writers had little knowledge of some of the societies they were reporting about, in terms of their history and political arrangement. What is sure is that some of them made an assumption or drew a conclusion based on preconceived notions they had already built about Africans. Moreover, the above information was penned down when the political structure of the people had been reorganized to fit into the overall European expansionist interest. What is historic about the Nikyob society is that it was like other groups within central Nigeria who were segmentary. Scholars have conveniently referred to them as non-centralized societies; this is to rightly describe their socio-political setup. What this nomenclature portends to historicizing their political development is that they never had a single political structure that united them into a large (single) polity, not until the advent of the British Indirect Rule.

Historically, political power resided in the hands of elders starting from the extended family to the clan, then the village and the entire community. There was also devolution of political authority across the component villages that made up the whole Nikyob group. No evidence exists of a strong central (single) authority wielding influence over the entire ethnic group. But each village had a council of elders that was made up of representatives of clan/lineage heads. This is the body that exercised both political and religious functions and whenever the need arose, acted as a judicial and legislative arm. There was never a defined precedent except that the council operated in a very democratic manner and each member participated fully and their views were respected. But in the case of the oldest member (*gbed*) of the council, the highest regard was given to his views placing him in a position to assume some form of headship over their sessions.[37] Intra-communal disputes were resolved by elders (representatives) from each side sitting together to arrive at a compromise.

---

[36]   NAK: ZAR PROF 1770; "Tribal and Administrative organization Report", by A.B. Matthews.

[37]   Abdullahi Oumar Musa Ashafa (Jnr), "An Unexplored State of the Sokoto Caliphate in Southern Zaria: A History of the Jema'a Emirate; C.1800-1967", (Unpublished B.A. Project, Bayero University, Kano, 1991), pp.5-6, 15-18; Yusufu Turaki, *The British Colonial Legacy*, pp. 43-48.

By and large, Nikyob had a wonderful/complex sociopolitical arrangement in which the various segments of society were held together by various rituals and practices which were overseen by the oldest man, a chief-priest, known as *Kyop-Ngban.*[38] He was the custodian of the history, culture, rites, and welfare of the entire society. In the Hausa Language, the closest term to it, for easy understanding is *Magajin Dodo.*[39] This arrangement survived until the British finally overran Nikyob Land and then tinkered with this rich cultural heritage.

iv.   Religious Worldview

Worldview generally is such a critical element in the life of every society. This is because it determines beliefs and consequently, the day-to-day intra-communal and inter-communal behaviors. Anything short of proper understanding, appreciating, and interpreting the worldview of Africans in general and Nikyob people in particular, will undoubtedly lead to a distorted analysis of their lives. Without fear of contradiction, it can be stated that it is practically impossible to rightly understand and interpret the past concerning current happenings without one having a good grasp of this solid heritage that holds the key to the deeper part of any society.[40]

Thus, a worldview is a set of a complex system of beliefs, basic assumptions, values, and allegiances with various interconnected variables built into daily lives and deeper than a culture that is on the surface level. When probed deeper, there are specific values that form the bedrock for the system of understanding the world. These values within their ideas and beliefs are inseparable, guiding choices and decisions that manifest in a group's judgment of others, issues, and events.[41]

---

[38]   Brief History of Bakin Kogi (Kyung) Kaninkon, Unpublished Manuscript, (n.d.), p. 4.

[39]   Brief History of Bakin Kogi (Kyung) Kaninkon, Unpublished Manuscript, (n.d.), p. 4.

[40]   Godwin Danjuma Kwalbe, Mikah Nuhu Adamu & Sulaiman I. Richifa, "An Appraisal of the African World View and Orthodox Medicine within Kafanchan Town, Kaduna State", in *POLAC International Journal of Economics and Management Science (PIJEMS), Vol.8, No.1, April 2022, ISSN: 2465-708*,. Department of Economics and Management Science Nigeria Police Academy, Kano, p. 366.

[41]   Godwin Danjuma Kwalbe, Mikah Nuhu Adamu & Sulaiman I. Richifa, "An Appraisal of the African World View and Orthodox Medicine within Kafanchan Town, Kaduna State", in *POLAC International Journal of Economics and Management Science (PIJEMS), Vol.8, No.1, April 2022, ISSN: 2465-7085,* Department of Economics and Management Science Nigeria Police Academy, Kano, pp. 366-367.

Over the years, some elements have become noticeable markers that can be easily identified while interrogating the Nikyob worldview in particular and Africa in general. The ones observed here are not in any way close to being exhaustive but appear to be common across the continent.

The average Nikyob was a committed member of his/her community-tribe, clan, or village. This sheds light on the value of relationships with other members of society. He/she abhorred individualism and seemed not to find fulfillment in being alone. He/she constantly found meaning in life within the community. Even when outside the community, he/she never ceases to see himself as an intricate member of that community. So also with the community, on the other hand, saw itself as part of the one member outside the ancestral land. However, today, due to increasing modernization and many people now living in cities where tribal bonds are very weak; many of these values have depreciated particularly the tenet of watching out for the good of one another.

Belief in God the Supreme Being came naturally to Nikyob children due to the series of initiation rites that have been discussed in the subsequent sections. They worshipped the supreme God even if they had no experiential knowledge of his personality. Religiosity was therefore synonymous with being a real man and as such, it can be said in other words that religion enveloped the entire content of their worldview with its manifestations in daily living. The weight of the influence of G(g)od hung so close.[42] Sadly, most Western scholars have erroneously concluded that Africans never believed in the supreme God. This is ignorance, to say the least, because traditional Nikyob people, from childhood, grew up with the knowledge of this Supreme Being referred to as *Rik*.[43] This supreme God was worshipped in the company of or through other deities. This is because the Supreme Being is transcendent and impersonal. Therefore he is to be approached through lesser and tangible gods. But today, due to the increasing rate of urbanization, conversion to Christianity, Islam, and new age religions, there is now disregard for the traditional religion/gods.

---

[42]   Yusufu Turaki, *The Trinity of Sin*, (Nairobi: HippoBooks, 2011), P.13. Matthew Hassan Kukah, *Religion, Politics and Power in Northern Nigeria*, (Ibadan: Spectrum Books Ltd, 1993), p. ix.

[43]   *Rik* is used interchangeably as the name for God Almighty and the sun. But in order to differentiate the Supreme Being from the mere element which gives out light, the sun is also called *nzang*. The implications here are that a) our ancestors must have probably worshipped the sun and b) they must have probably had a knowing of the existence of a being beyond the sky and that he was different from an inanimate element. See, Bauta D. Motty, *Indigenous Christian*, p. 134.

Similarly, along with the belief in a Supreme Being and the worship of several deities, there was high knowledge and awareness of spirits. For the average Nikyob person, the whole of nature is saturated with spirits[44] who are in constant activities around and collaboration with members of the community. Some of these spirits are agents of evil while some are responsible for good. Certain trees, valleys, forests, mountains, rivers, etc. are designated as natural habitats of the spirits. To approach these places, it has to be by permission or through offerings to appease these spirits. This notion of spirit was so widespread in their belief system. As they moved out of their ancestral land, they carried with them this belief into the city. They held on to the idea of spirits hovering everywhere and impacting the lives of people in the community.[45] To the average member of society, nothing is dead or inactive as held in science. The rocks and rivers for instance are not just mere elements in the ecosystem but full members and agents of good and evil whenever they are taken over by evil or good spirits.

Closely linked to this, is the belief in witchcraft. Witches are members of society with supernatural abilities to cause harm or misfortune to others. Every unpleasant occurrence, disaster, and tragedy is quietly explained as the result of the activities of witches. The law of cause and effect is not given expression among many traditional members of a community. It is just the normal thing to point to the activities of witchcraft in the community when confronted with pain and sorrow. Nothing sufficiently explained why bad things happened to good people except that the bad witches were responsible.[46] Some also believed in the existence of good witches who do not cause harm or do evil to members of society. They only use their witchcraft to defend their families, bring good to their families, and see when evil is being hatched to raise alarm.

The consequence of the foregoing mindset is that in the face of tragedy (illness and death), the acceptable thing to do is to query the cause in terms of who did it. This can be appreciated whenever issues of terminal illnesses, epidemics, and imminent death are battled with in the village. The question is always, by default, who did it and not what caused it? The latter is scientific and does not sufficiently meet the needs of this society based on its worldview.

Another heavy and real element within the worldview is the concept of ancestors. These are the spirits of the dead members of a family/clan

---

44   Yusufu Turaki, *The Trinity of Sin*, p. 10.
45   Karl Grebe and Wilfred Fon, *African Traditional Religion and Christian Counselling*, (India: Oasis international Limited, 2007), p. 9.
46   Samuel Waje Kunhiyop, *African Christian Theology*. (Nairobi: HippoBooks, 2012), pp. 212 – 214.

to which one belongs. This belief is an intricate part of the religious life of Africans. Ancestors are highly talked about and venerated through rituals and sacrifices. Through words and actions, no one tolerates disrespect for ancestors, and constant fellowship with these relatives is maintained and anticipated.[47] Ancestors remain part of the community and the daily lives of members. They are not a forgotten past but constant players in the social and religious lives with huge mediatory roles with the gods. With this overview of worldview, it is now easy to understand the socio-cultural and religious life of the Ninkyob people. This is necessary because the life of a Nikyob person was not compartmentalized; that is to say, you could not separate religion from culture, economy, politics, marriage, etc. these were all intertwined.

v.   Cultural Practices and Initiation Rites

Kinship and Ancestry

Among the Nikyob people, in pre-colonial and post-colonial contexts, kinship is very strong and does not only exist for social relationships but is part of the emotional and economic support system. What is also obvious is that Nikyob society was patriarchal. The man or the head of a family plays a central role whenever decision-making is being contemplated. Critical matters and lingering crises are settled at his final pronouncement. Aside from the nuclear family unit, the extended family system was a continuum of the social organization and mostly did not only revolve around bloodline but even strangers who have stayed long enough on the property of a particular family, eventually became assimilated into their benefactor's family or clan and by this enlarges the kinship unit.

Marriage

Marriage among Nikyob people is a much-esteemed institution and it is recognized to occur between two adults (male and female) with both social and biological significance. Socially, it was a collective responsibility of members of the family, clan, and society to help one secure a partner and also ensure the union succeeds. Refusal to partake in this union was considered

---

[47]   Duncan Olumbe, "African Worldview: An introduction", July 2008. Retrieved from https:///wa-tumishiwaneno.files.wordpress.com/2014/08/African_worlview_introduction.pdf (21-09-2021).

an abnormality and even a curse to the individual. Biologically, it was seen as the medium for procreation; that is why bareness was loathed. The process commences with a series of negotiations between the groom's and bride's families aimed at solidifying a lifelong and solid bond beyond the couple.[48]

The marriage rites begin the same day a female child is born into to a family. The first parent to arrive at the house would fix a stick of broom or a feather in the girl's hair as a proclamation of their interest in having her as a wife for their son. This act was technically referred to as *Niak-Nkwa*, it was a practice meant to preserve the sanctity of marriage and to shield the younger generation from unnecessary mistakes. It also shows the level of trust children had in their parents to make such a great decision on their behalf. As soon as the deal (*Niak-Nkwa*) is put in place, the proposing parents would go further to seal it by offering a hoe to the family of the bride-in-waiting.[49] This can be understood as a message that agriculture was central to the daily lives of the Nikyob family. It also underpins the purpose of marriage for procreation to invariably have enough hands in the farmlands. The gift to the family of the girl continues up to marriage and beyond in the forms of labor during farming, food items, chickens, goats, etc. these are the items that were defined as the bride price in Nikyob pre-colonial society. As the relations advanced, the interactions between the two families were shouldered by a woman from the boy's family who was married into the girl's family. She practically goes between the two sides taking and delivering messages. She was referred to as *whah tyeh zhiyol.*[50]

The wedding ceremony was usually elaborate and characterized by the joyous celebration from everyone around through a great feast made up of varieties of meat, drinks, and food. The historical import here is that hospitality has been part and parcel of this society.[51] However, it should be stated here that society was patriarchal. Conversely, one's family consisted of his father's and mother's relatives; hence sexual and marital relationship was forbidden between these paternal and maternal family members. Also, divorce occurred in Nikyob society but always as a result of unresolved cases of impotence, bareness, deprivation of sex, and other myriads of unaccepted behaviors.[52]

---

[48]   Bauta D. Motty, *Indigenous Christian*, pp. 141-142.

[49]   Brief History of Bakin Kogi (Kyung) Kaninkon, Unpublished Manuscript, (n.d.), p. 9.

[50]   Bauta D. Motty, *Indigenous Christian*, p. 143.

[51]   A lot about the institution of marriage in Ninkyob society has been dealt with by Professor Bauta D. Motty in his *Indigenous Christian Disciple-Making.*

[52]   Brief History of Bakin Kogi (Kyung) Kaninkon, Unpublished Manuscript, (n.d.), p. 11.

Initiations

A new born was usually welcomed with great celebration by both parents and other members of the extended family and community. The birth of a child was considered a sign of a blessing in the marriage. There was no great ceremony attached to naming a new born but the names were specially chosen to reflect past and future events or even to respond to prevailing circumstances at the point of the child's birth. This can be seen in the list of names given by parents, grandparents (maternal and paternal), etc., names like: Tyokpak, Nikyu, Kon, Renet, Veh-Yah, Borl and others.

The process of initiation was complex for the male members of society. It began with a hunting expedition for rodents surrounding the immediate community. This was a deliberate attempt to introduce the youngsters to the disciplines of hard work and endurance in preparation for circumcision between the ages of eight and nine with circumcision carried out afterward. The series of initiations in Nikyob Land had been exhaustively researched and documented by Rev. Prof. Bauta D. Motty.[53] The interesting thing to note at this point is that the life of a Nikyob man, from birth to death was wrapped in a series of initiations from one stage to another and several rituals for purification and cleansing for man to strike a balance (peacefully coexist) with nature and fellow man.[54]

Child Naming

Naming a child was never a casual exercise but something which had a connection to the family ancestry, circumstances of birth, and prayers/wishes for the future. It was rare to have an individual with a single name as a new born was a delight to all members of the lineage and the community. Therefore, the usual practice was that the immediate parents of the child would give their desired names, older relations would give their own, and grandparents were also always involved. The result was that everyone called the child by his/her preferred name and this was never a problem to society.[55]

---

53 See, Bauta D. Motty, *Indigenous Christian,* pp. 154-162.
54 Bauta D. Motty, *Indigenous Christian,* pp. 163-185
55 Bauta D. Motty, Indigenous Christian, pp. 157-158

Education and Socialization

Indigenous education in Nikyob land was designed to raise disciplined and self-reliant members of the society. The general practice was that boys spent most of their time with fathers or men and were practically mentored to take over responsibilities or occupations of their fathers. In the same vein, girls grew up under the tutorship of their mothers and other older women in the family and society at large. For the most part, the education was informal except for secluded moments of intensive instruction, like initiation ceremonies. A good example is the circumcision rites which were elaborate and well-structured. It can pass for what we refer to today as formal education because it was deliberate and had clear goals and objectives. Within this general Nikyob traditional mode of education, taboos were used as social control mechanisms especially as they had contained in them, consequences. The regulations were on three levels - economic (conservation of the environment and natural resources), social (guidelines for interpersonal relationships), and religious (unity or harmony between the physical world and the supernatural.[56]

vi.   Changing Demographics in the Nineteenth Century

Culturally speaking, the entire composition of the population within Nikyob area can be said to be monolithic in the early times. This remained as such for a long period until the second half of the 18th century[57] when the population started experiencing transformation in terms of its diversity. This began with the steady seasonal migration of the Fulani herders and Hausa traders. The reason for this new phase is traceable to the abundance of economic opportunities;[58] this location supports a wide variety of food and cash crops. Its climatic condition is also suitable for both human habitation and quality livestock. Huge solid minerals in high quality and quantity have been identified and even explored. For the sake of emphasis, this geographical information is vital to understanding how this area became an attraction for various groups in pre-colonial and post-colonial times.

---

56 Bauta D. Motty, *Indigenous Christian*, pp. 158-172.
57 Simon Yohanna, *The National Question: Ethnic Minorities and Conflicts in Northern Nigeria*, (Kagoro: Mikrom Prints, 2008), pp. 146-147.
58 Abdullahi Oumar Musa Ashafa (Jnr), "An Unexplored State of the Sokoto Caliphate in Southern Zaria: A History of the Jema'a Emirate; C.1800-1967", (Unpublished B.A. Project, Bayero University, Kano, 1991), pp. 2-4; Gaius Jatau, *The Colonial Economy of Jema'a*, p. 20.

The primary occupation of these Hausa settlers was trading, while the bulk of the Fulani settlers were pastoralists with only temporary shelters just for a particular season. For instance, the pastoralists moved in a regular pattern - a southerly direction, primarily in search of green pasture and water for their flocks. However, with the approach of the wet season, the direction of the movement changed northward; that is, they moved back to their original point of setting out.[59] Trade was well established in this area as there was recorded, firsthand by Lander in 1827 when he visited and found the entire axis a flourishing trade center with Europeans, Arabs, and Africans exchanging such articles as rings, honey, needles, clothes, animal skins, agricultural produce, and slaves.[60] In furtherance of the mercantile economy around this region, there existed a renowned trade route that linked it with Hausa land. This route was part of the Trans-Saharan trade route passing through Zaria, then Jama'a, Keffi, Nasarawa, Lafia, Doma, and the Benue Valley. This route was very significant as it served as a bridge between the far north and the inhabitants of this area. The long-term implications of all this foregoing discussion are that the population of the whole area including that of Nikyob became mixed. With time, the socio-political organization of these host groups was altered permanently without recourse to its previous historical arrangement.

vii. Economic Activities

Agriculture was the bed rock of the Nikyob economy. The early people were farmers who were able to explore, subdue, and exploit their natural environment. This is consistent with the argument by Simon Yohanna that a survey of the general environment in Southern Kaduna shows sufficient evidence that intense human activities have altered the vegetation:

> In the first place, the vegetation of the area is already man-made. Issues like the seasonal nomadic activities of the Fulani, the vagaries of the weather, the soils cannot be said to be serious enough factors to result in the present state of vegetation. A trip from Kagoro…through Kwoi, Kagoma,

---

[59] Godwin Danjuma Kwalbe, "The Evolution and Development of Kafanchan; 1927-1960. (Unpublished B. A. Project, A.B.U. Zaria), pp. 13-14.

[60] C.L. Temple, *Tribes, Provinces, Emirates and States of the Northern Provinces of Nigeria*, (London: Frank Cass and Co. Ltd. 1965), p. 517.

Tsakiya, Jaban Kogo, Kachia, Geshere to Saminaka shows clearly the extent to which the vegetation has seriously been altered due perhaps, to centuries or millennia of man's activities.[61]

This being the case, it is safe to state that the Nikyob people along with their Southern Kaduna neighbors have long transited from the hunting and gathering stage of the early form of human socio-economic activity and have adopted the sedentary lifestyle which is stable and a higher form of civilization. Hence, farming different varieties of food crops (grains, vegetables, fruits, and roots) was well entrenched. Again, a high level of advancement was noticed in the agriculture sector within Nikyob society. For instance, the modern idea of shifting cultivation and crop rotation was well practiced in their early days. Nonproductive lands (discovered through low yields either as a result of poor soil fertility or as a result of long-term use) were abandoned for new ones.[62] The wealth of the society was not measured in monetary terms as it (currency) did not exist nor was needed. Apart from the number of wives and children, a rich man was known for the size of his farmlands and harvest. Incidentally, the two factors impacted one another.

Besides crop production, animal husbandry featured in the economy of Nikyob society. Animals ranging from goats, dogs, fowls, etc. were raised to supplement the dietary portions of the people. These animals were also more than just part of the food but also served as elements in the ritual practices of the society. Therefore, their existence and usefulness cannot be quantified. Certain payments within the socio-cultural practices were demanded in the forms of goats or fowls thereby making their existence necessary in every household.

Hunting was also part of the economy. It was common in the dry season when people finished their farm work. It was done on a communal basis; the philosophy behind this was very beautiful. A single individual would not be able to confront the wild beasts; therefore, it was normal to practice this in a period when everyone was available. Apart from getting food supplements, this practice was used to further push away some of the ferocious beasts already encroaching on the surrounding settlement. Fishing was also central and practiced in the same way hunting was done. It was in the dry season

---

[61]   Simon Yohanna, "Southern Zaria in Historical Perspectives", A Paper Presented in Room 79, F.A.S.S. Building, A.B.U Zaria, 1982, p. 8.

[62]   Rev. (Barr.) Wakili Kadima, interviewed at Jos Street, Kafanchan (10/12/2012).

when the water level dropped thereby making all the fishing methods adopted to be result-oriented.

Handcrafts supplied the other essential articles used at home or farm. By this, the society is said to have operated a self-sufficient economy. They produced what they needed and used the resources at their disposal. But as society became integrated, interdependence was naturally inculcated. This led the Nikyob people away from a subsistence economy to the stage of capital acquisition introduced at the end of the nineteenth and beginning of the twentieth centuries through British mercantile interests and the subsequent colonial conquest.

viii.   Arts and Entertainment

Arts and entertainment are a part of the daily lives of humanity. Every society has developed its ways and instruments for transmitting messages concerning the event being celebrated. Most of these instruments for musical purposes were made from animal skins, bones, horns, tree trunks, barks, and cornstalks. Some of them were for light relaxation in the evenings within the neighborhood, mostly during the dry season when farm work has reduced. Major festivities were the *dung* which involved a larger segment or whole community with a lot of dance and feasting.

An individual can organize a mini-festivity (*Ntwam)*. This may involve initiation, funerals, weddings, etc. The evenings were strictly for entertainment across the age groups with grandparents seizing the opportunity to instill moral values into their grandchildren via stories and folktales. Nikyob people were known for two categories of styles of dance - *mbaya* and *zyor-mma*.[63] The bottom line is that life among Nikyob people was not all hard work, but they had time for entertainment and relaxation.

ix.   Inter-Group Relations

Ample information exists to prove that the Nikyob people had robust inter-group relations with their long-term neighbors and later settlers. The available facts of history indicate that they have accommodated visitors from all walks of life. For instance, within the context of resisting human/slave

---

[63]   Yahaya Emmanuel Banang, "Kaninkon (Nikyob) Society: Historical and Contemporary Perspectives", (n.d., unpublished).

raiders and jihadists' expansions, the Nikyob group had jointly embarked on wars to push back the invaders. Oral account has also fully captured this rich history by stating that due to the defensive advantage enjoyed by the Kagoro people made possible by the massive hills, they (Nikyob) usually took their wives and children for safety among Kagoro settlements before facing the enemy in battle. Eventually, some stayed back and got integrated into the Kagoro society. For instance, the settlement of Tsonje in Kagoro was initially made up of Nikyob people from Sonje who came down the hills after the war against the jihadists but felt no need to return home. Also, in 1833, both Nikyob and Kagoro jointly defeated the invading force of jihadists. This is very interesting as it demonstrates the kind of trust and fraternity that existed between these two groups long before British forces integrated the different units under a single foreign administration system of Indirect Rule.[64]

In a similar display of camaraderie in 1915, Nikyob men got wind of the withdrawal of the British forces and attacked the emir of Jama'a and his team who were on tour to collect taxes from the Kaje people whom they (Nikyob) considered as their kinsmen, and because they saw the taxation under the emir as oppression by strangers. This particular event was a revolt against a system - British Indirect Rule and not against a religion or any ethnic group.

Similarly, a Kagoma traditional leader was arrested and detained in police custody for "rebellious" attitudes concerning the existing authority of the emir. This was in 1949; then, on thirteenth August of that same year, a band of Nikyob men under the leadership of Tete Kaninkon went to the police and demanded the release of the *Sarkin Fadan* Kagoma. There is no better uncovering here than the fact that these two groups have long considered themselves as one in pre-colonial times and saw the oppression of one group was considered as a collective problem to be solved by all.[65]

Additionally, at the early stage of the arrival of the Hausa traders and Fulani pastoralists, some of them made their way into Nikyob land and had productive economic relationships with them. Despite being in the minority, they were welcome and accommodated by their host. This is better appreciated when one considers that they started coming in small numbers and could not have posed a threat or muster enough courage to resist being exterminated by a warrior ethnic group like the Nikyob. This is clearly portrayed in the

---

[64]   Rev. (Barr.) Wakili Kadima, Interview, Kafanchan, 17-04-2022. Age-67; Kaninkon Development Association (KADA), "Memorandum to the Judicial Panel of Enquiry into the Kafanchan Crisis of May 22nd, 1999: The Position of the Kaninkon Community", p. 3.

[65]   NAK ZAR PROF. C. 28 Vol. II "Jama'a Division Affairs".

evolution of the Jama'a emirate with its seat, first sited at Jama'a-na-Roro (Jama'a of Roro), the present site of Gidan Waya, among Nikyob in their land. Since no record exists of an attack against the elements of the emirate by the Nikyob people; this further demonstrates their commitment to peaceful intergroup cooperation.[66]

x.   Nikyob History and Jama'a Emirate

The history of the Jama'a Emirate can be traced to the gradual migration of the Fulanis into the entire Southern Kaduna area and Nikyob land in particular which began around the eighteenth century. By the end of the nineteenth century, permanent Fulani settlements emerged as well as the establishment of the institution of the *Ardo*. However, this leadership structure was only within the Fulani stock. Interestingly, some of them decided to stay outside this pseudo-political structure and its influence. This is clearly understood in the light of the new home they found. For instance, their lives and properties were not under any threat from the indigenous groups; as such, they could choose to live their lives free of the new political institution that was evolving and taking the appearance of an exclusively Fulani political structure. The factor of common language provided a mutual bond among the Fulani settlers until later, when the whole arrangement changed with the coming of one Mallam Usman Kebbi.[67]

Mallam Usman was an Islamic preacher who was permitted to preach outside Zaria among Fulani pastoralists who had settled in scattered groups by the Kachecheri Plateau. He worked his way into becoming accepted and trusted by his relatives leading to their patronage of his religious insights on issues of their daily lives. This also placed him in a position to arbitrate in non-religious (civil) matters, thereby making him a threat to the *Sarkin* Kajuru, who had earlier enjoyed unrivaled authority amongst the settlers with the backing of Zaria. All these political transformations took place when the Fulani Jihadists overthrew the *Habe* rulers at Zaria. This revolution which successfully replaced the *Habe* rulers with a new set of participants of the Fulani breed sent negative signals to the Kajuru rulers, who genuinely became apprehensive of their Fulani neighbors that were being galvanized

---

[66]   Godwin Danjuma Kwalbe,"The Evolution and Development of Kafanchan; 1927-1960", (Unpublished B.A. Project, A.B.U, Zaria, 2006), pp. 22-23.

[67]   Godwin Danjuma Kwalbe, "The Evolution and Development of Kafanchan", pp. 15-17.

into a united force. However, they were at the same time encouraged by the successes recorded by their kinsmen, especially in Zaria.

The immediate step taken by Kajuru to maintain its uninterrupted dominance was a plot to eliminate the perceived danger. This secret plan was said to have been revealed to the Fulanis, leading to their escape at night, moving westward to the edge of the Kagoro Plateau, and settling finally on the spur of the Daroro Hills in Nikyob land. The consequence of this migration was that the escaping Fulani pushed away the indigenous people they met in the area who built the village of present-day Nindem. However, this did not put the dream to terminate this new threat by Kajuru to rest because another attempt was made but halted at Kwakwasa. The aftermath of this defeat was the dispersal of the Kajuru elements to Keffi and the emergence (transformation) of a new political atmosphere.[68]

It must be stated, for the sake of emphasis, that before this period of upheaval, a cordial relationship existed between the non-Fulani people of Kajuru and the Fulani settlers who were scattered around the Kachechere Plateau. This is true since one of the wives of the *Sarkin* Kajuru was Fulani. She was even the person who leaked the plot to annihilate Mallam Usman Kebbi.

Equally, the fleeing band of the Fulanis under the leadership of Mallam Usman did not think of going to Zaria for safety but preferred to go into Nikyob land. It was also a combined force of the Fulanis and Nikyob men who defeated the Kajuru at Kwakwasa - an excellent intergroup cooperation. Furthermore, Mallam Usman was hosted by Da-Roro a Nikyob man. "Dah-Roro" literally means brother Roro, which was used over time and merged into one word as his name. He was much-admired for having offered Usman accommodation with a space for his religious prayers and convenient quarters to attend to his guests.[69] This was a relationship that transcended ethnic and religious divides.

Furthermore, the emergence of the Jama'a political institution, which was always traced to C.1810, was not a result of the special effort of the Fulani settlers alone. The name "Jama'a" came when Mallam Usman Kebbi in the company of Nikyob men and other natives went to Zaria to ask for a flag of recognition, and the emir of Zaria Mallam Musa inquired who they were, and Usman replied that they were a party of a gathering of people who had settled close to the mountain of Daroro. Consequently, the emir of Zaria [re]named

[68] A.H.M. Kirk-Greene, *Gazetteers of Northern Provinces of Nigeria, Vol.III; The Central Kingdoms,* *(London*: Frank Cass and Co. Ltd., 1972), p. 13.

[69] A. H. M. Kirk-Greene, *Gazetteers of Northern Provinces of Nigeria,* p. 13.

the area Jama'a-Daroro (the group or party of Da-Roro).[70] What this means is that there would not have been Jama'a Emirate as we have it today without the effort of Roro a Nikyob man.

It may also interest the reader to note that much of the history of the Jama'a Emirate has been misrepresented for the sake of advancing a particular group's interest at the expense of others. Most writers of the history of Southern Zaria have always argued that there was the occurrence of a Jihad in this area in 1810 which then led to the emergence of an emirate called Jama'a. This particular emirate is the only Muslim-model political institution among the predominantly non-Muslim peoples. The emergence of the Jama'a political institution was not a result of the singular effort of the Fulani settlers alone as has been demonstrated above. It is not historically correct to say that it was formed in 1810. For instance, M. G. Smith believes, in his writings that Jama'a was not an emirate right from 1810 but was only made an emirate by the British in 1902.[71] His argument is based on the fact that all the emirates were recognized at Sokoto and not Zaria; hence Jama'a did not qualify for the title of an emirate at this early date (1810). In the same vein, Salisu Bala does not believe that the activity which led to the emergence of Jama'a-Da-Roro qualifies to be called a Jihad. This is because the indigenous people joined forces with Mallam Usman to defeat Mallam Haruna, the *Sarkin* Kajuru who was a threat to both settlers and indigenous peoples. Besides, the issuance of a flag, in this case, was done after a battle had been successfully fought and won unlike in the case of the emergence of other emirates under the Sokoto Caliphate where the issuance of a flag at Sokoto preceded the execution of any war (Jihad).[72] This argument and position along with Smith's are very reasonable. M. G. Smith lived within this area (Kagoro to be specific) for some years before returning home.[73] Thus, his views are that of one nearer to the source. There is a high chance that he interviewed people who were closer to eye witnesses of events in this area.

In doing a critical reflection, a combined force of Muslims and non-Muslims could not have fought in a war (Jihad) to advance the course of Islam. This practice was never common and cannot be substantiated anywhere. It is rather safe to call this a war of liberation from the clutches of Kajuru in the

---

[70]   A. H. M. Kirk-Greene, *Gazetteers of Northern Provinces of Nigeria*, p. 16.

[71]   M.G. Smith, *Government in Zazzau*, (Oxford University Press, 1960), pp. 138-140.

[72]   Salisu Bala, "Kafanchan Communal Conflict 1985: A Critical Analysi of the Causes", A Paper Presented at N.D.A. Kaduna", 2006, P.9.

[73]   Yusufu Turaki, *The British Colonial Legacy*, p. 23.

form of slave raiding or an attempt by Fulani elements to carve out a political space for themselves. The name Jama'a as we have seen emerged when a group of Fulani Muslims and indigenous peoples introduced themselves before the emir of Zaria. It is logical to put Jama'a in a different historical scenario and not to be taken together with those emirates that were set up directly as a result of Usman dan Fodio's jihad. Furthermore, Sa'ad Abubakar has authoritatively informed that the Jihad officially came to an end in 1809 but efforts to establish new political enclaves as part of the caliphate continued in non-Hausa places even up to the 1820s especially for British administrative convenience, in places like Nupe, Illorin and a decade later, Misau and Jama'are emerged. Then Kontagoro was established in 1859.[74] This is the category that Jama'a falls under.

Furthermore, a greater part of the Middle-Belt and Southern Zaria in particular has no evidence of being successfully overrun by the Fulani forces. Continuous resistance to the incursion of the jihadists was sustained up to the arrival of the British and the establishment of its so-called Indirect Rule System. The evidence shows an unsuccessful attempt to conquer them in pre-colonial times.[75]

In addition, there was no central political unit that was conquered to be replaced with a government in the Islamic model. To further appreciate this historical fact, it is important to note the actions of the British in the process of time when colonial rule had been fully established. The British took a step to reduce the influence of Zaria by severing Jama'a from it. The British would not have separated Jama'a from Zaria in 1902 and made it a Division under Nasarawa Province as punishment to Zaria for its complicity in the death of Captain Moloney if not that it was involved in its formation. The imperialists demonstrated some great sense of respect for the existing structure of the Sokoto Caliphate.[76] Strictly speaking, from available evidence, the Jama'a Emirate is a British colonial creation; it was never an emirate in the sense of the tradition of other emirates in Northern Nigeria. This was confirmed by a British officer in a report:

---

[74]   Sa'ad Abubakar, "The Established Caliphate: Sokoto, the Emirates and their Neighbours" , in Ikime, O. *Groundwork of Nigerian History* (Ibadan: Heinemann Educational Books (Nigeria) Plc., 1999), pp.303-326.

[75]   T. G. O. Gbadamosi & J.F.Ade Ajayi, "Islam and Christianity in Nigeria", in Ikime, Obaro. *Groundwork of Nigerian History* (Ibadan: Heinamann Education Books (Nigeria) Plc., 1999), pp. 347-366.

[76]   S. J. Hogben and A.H.M. Kirk-Greene, *The Emirates of Northern Nigeria; A Preliminary Survey of their Historical Traditions,* (London: Oxford University Press, 1966), p. 554.

"In September, 1911, an independent holding letter was
granted among others, the Emir of Jama'a appointing him
formally Emir of 2nd class status"[77]

Outstandingly, this report provides sufficient information to conclude
that the Emirate of Jama'a came as a child of necessity because the indigenous
peoples of Southern Zaria had no central political power structure that
the British could depend on for effective administration of the whole area.
Since the imperial interest was expedient, this innovation was the solution.
The innovation was given a tentative trial in 1902 and formalized in 1911
as contained in the report above. This British imposition of Muslim-style
administration over the peoples of Southern Zaria was vehemently rejected in
words and actions. On 27th January 1933, the Chief of Ayu, in a memorandum
to E.S. Pembleton who was Resident Officer of Plateau Province, stated that: "I
no longer wish to remain under the Fulanis by whom we were never conquered
and whom my forefather, Abukum, defeated".[78]

The contempt over Jama'a Emirate was not only from the indigenous
peoples but even the British, who were its architects saw through and regretted
their action that was not yielding the desired results but rather became a
burden to them. Therefore, on 1st November 1935 when E.S. Pembleton was
submitting a report to his superior officer, Secretary, Northern Province, he
recommended among other things that:

> My recommendations in brief, are: (i) Jema'a Emirate should
> continue to be administered as at present until the office
> of Emir falls vacant when separate Native Administrations
> should be formed for the pagan communities... (ii) I have
> endeavoured to show above that the continuance of Fulani
> rule in most of the area is not in accord with the declared
> policy of Government and that there is good reason for
> abolishing it.[79]

At this point, we are now being furnished with concrete facts informing
the reader that Jama'a Emirate was purely a British creation. The usual
practice back then was for the imperialists to depose any recalcitrant emir

---

[77] NAK NAS PROF: "Quarterly Report Ended 31st March, 1913".
[78] KADA, "Memorandum to the Judicial Panel of Enquiry into the Kafanchan Crisis of May, 22nd,
      1999: The Position of the Kaninkon Community." n.d.
[79] KADA. "Memorandum to the Judicial Panel of Enquiry into the Kafanchan Crisis of May, 22nd,
      1999: The Position of the Kaninkon Community." n.d., p.11.

or traditional ruler. It was not common to contemplate complete dissolution because they promised to honor the structure they made on the ground.[80] But to indulge this line of action, we have sufficient grounds to conclude that it was their project. Consistent with the British colonial practice, maximizing profit at all costs was top on their priority list. Hence, when the Southern Zaria region presented them with a complex situation, crafting an emirate that never existed became a solution. Once more, Sa'ad Abubakar gives us reasons to stand on this line of thought:

> ...the traditional system of government varied from one area to another. There was also the problem of ethnic diversity. Thus it was impossible to recognize the numerous petty socio-political units as they had existed for the purpose of provincial and divisional administrations. In trying to establish some sort of administration over the diverse heterogonous peoples, the British felt that the 'emirate type' organization was the best answer. Consequently, the larger states in the region were constituted into emirates. Thus, the Hausa states of Yawuri, Kebbi and Abuja became emirates and their rulers styled emirs... there were also within the Middle Belt region a number of states which were dependencies of some emirates. Zaria for example was in control of Keffi, Doma, **Jama'a** and Nasarawa (my emphasis)...[81]

This view above strengthens the argument so far and also refutes the popular opinion that Jama'a emirate emerged in 1810 and was a direct result of the greater Jihad of Usman dan Fodio which scholars like Abubakar have situated between 1804-1809. Jama'a was only a dependency of Zaria until the British found it expedient to make it an emirate. Therefore, with this revelation, the rich history of the Jama'a Emirate should only be celebrated in the light of unity and collaboration from culturally diverse people as against the sole effort of Fulani/Muslims.

---

[80] Sa'ad Abubakar, *The Established Caliphate*, p. 451.
[81] Sa'ad Abubakar, *The Established Caliphate*, pp. 457-458.

xi.   Dangoma in Nikyob History

The settlement of Dangoma offers another exciting history in terms of positive intergroup relations in Nikyob history. Situated within Nikyob land, it is bounded by Goska to the north, Bakin Kogi to the west, Amere, and Gerti to the south, and Gidan Waya and Nindem to the east. It was made up of ex-slaves liberated from the Fulani oppression by Nikyob and Kagoro. They usually accompanied them (Fulani) to loot those things left (considered unattractive) by their Fulani lords during raids. Their oral tradition exaggerates their existence in the area as far back as the early fifteenth century.[82] But this is falsehood only invented to acquire the status of being original to the site. This view has no historical backing especially when one sees that they do not have any cultural or linguistic affinity with the surrounding groups.

For religion, they practice Islam and speak Fulfulde, making them identify themselves as Fulani. But physically, they are not of Fulani stock. However, due to their years of subjection to the Fulani as enslaved people, they have lost their identity hence the adoption of a new identity as Fulani, which is understandably a form of continued loyalty.[83] From available records (oral and written), their liberation occurred in 1903[84] with an offer of accommodation in their present site within Kaninkon Chiefdom. On the other hand, the oral tradition among Nikyob people states that they were ten (10) in numbers but grew through births and immigrants. This data shows that Dangoma translates to ten persons in the Hausa language (dan-goma).[85] This account is reliable because it comes from the host community that had long inhabited the area before the liberation and settlement of the people of Dangoma. More so, they are surrounded by Nikyob settlements suggesting that they were kept in a strategic position (safe) to avoid any danger, particularly from their erstwhile lords. Till today, they are treated as an extension of Nikyob society without segregation. Their population today also gives insight into this. They are just a small fraction of the entire population of Kaninkon Chiefdom.

---

[82]   Alhaji Waje Damina (Dangaladiman Dangoma). Interview, a retired army officer, 81 years old. 28-12-2016.

[83]   Result of the researcher's fieldwork.

[84]   A.H.M. Kirk-Greene, *Gazetteers of the Northern Provinces of Nigeria, Volume III: The Central Kingdoms (Kontagora, Nasarawa, Nupe, Ilorin)*, (London: Frank Cass, 1972), p. 15.

[85]   Godwin Danjuma Kwalbe, "Re-Southern Kaduna Muslim Ummah Development Association (SOKAMUDA): Letter of advise on recurring communal Disturbances in Southern Kaduna Particularly recent ones in Kajuru, Zangon-Kataf and Kajuru Local Government Areas of Kaduna State", 16th July 2020.

Overall, the foregoing discussion furnishes us with sufficient proof that healthy interactions existed with serious concessions extended to visitors. The inhabitants of Dangoma were few at the early stage and could have been easily exterminated by their host, assuming they were not welcome. Furthermore, to hold the view that the British government protected them all is not logical because the attainment of independence could have spelled doom to the existence of this settlement. As it is, they have never been threatened but instead they have been integrated into Nikyob society as a unit. This is an excellent history of intergroup cooperation in the area. Unfortunately, this has remained unknown for easy politicization of poorly managed differences.[86]

---

[86] Godwin Danjuma Kwalbe, "Re-Southern Kaduna Muslim Ummah Development Association (SOKAMUDA): Letter of advise on recurring communal Disturbances in Southern Kaduna Particularly recent ones in Kajuru, Zangon-Kataf and Kajuru Local Government Areas of Kaduna State", 16th July 2020.

SECTION TWO: COLONIAL PERIOD

CHAPTER THREE:
COLONIAL CONQUEST

British Colonial Conquest of Nikyob Land and Resistance

For the Nikyob people as in the case of other groups in this zone, the journey to colonial subjugation started way back in the year 1900. This was when the flag of the Royal Niger Company gave way to the Union Jack of Great Britain; this was precisely in January 1900 under the leadership of Lieutenant-Colonel F.D. Lugard, the High Commissioner.[87] However, this declaration by Great Britain did not translate into an immediate loss of independence by the Nigerian people. But it, however, signaled the beginning. For the centralized Hausa states of the Sokoto Caliphate, it took a period of three years (1900-1903) for most of them to fall under the British invading forces.[88] The story was different for Nikyob society due to the obvious fact that it was not a centralized political structure that would have made the work easier like in the emirates. The other reason for the staggered nature of the British conquest is the factor of geography. Unlike their northern neighbors who were occupying flat and grassland areas, here, the land is punctuated by many hills and mountains with woodland forests that served as hideouts for the people.[89]

However, since the colonial enterprise was paramount, it became necessary for economic and strategic reasons to go out after it. After the formal submission, in March 1903 by the Emirs of Lafia and Jama'a, the British posted an Assistant Resident to Jama'a in October 1904. He was accompanied by a detachment of 25 rank and files under a subaltern.[90] But as would be expected, the various natives considered this invasion as a violation of their territorial integrity and fundamental human rights and therefore, resisted vehemently

---

[87] Yusufu Turaki, *The British Colonial Legacy*, p. 74.
[88] Yusufu Turaki, *The British Colonial Legacy*, p. 74.
[89] NAK: NAS PROF, December Quarterly Report 1915, pp.12-13.
[90] C.G. Ames, "The Central Kingdoms (Kontagora, Nasarawa, Nupe, Ilorin)", *in Gazetteers of the Northern Provinces of Nigeria, Volume III*,(London: Frank Cass, 1972), p. 19.

the attempt to occupy them. This action was countered by the destruction of lives and property without a second thought. Most settlements at this time were completely burnt down and people were taken away as war captives.[91] This brutal and punitive strategy succeeded in weakening the resistance being put up against the British invading forces. However, it should be noted that sustained resistance continued into the later days of colonial rule. It took the British over twenty years to carry out punitive patrols and tax enforcement in this area as its major activity without having firm military and political control over these independent polities.[92]

To maintain its presence among these diverse groups, the British government came up with a strategy which was to create an emirate in 1902, and made it a Division under Nasarawa Province to coordinate political affairs in the area consistent with the philosophy of Indirect Rule. This action was followed up with an authorization letter from the colonial government in 1911.[93] In particular reference to Nikyob society, the colonial project was a very difficult one for both the British and Jama'a Emirate, their accomplice in the Indirect Rule. The resistance to the foreign occupation was fierce and prolonged because of the determination from both sides never to give up. The British colonial officers were not always around but visited routinely to ensure compliance with their instructions. What this meant is that the elements of the emirate often bear the brunt of the grievances expressed by the Nikyob people and their neighbors. For instance, in 1915, a report offered insight into the nature of reaction against minority rule:

> The Emir was on an ordinary ceremonial tour and when camped at Togwoi received visits from various village heads. The Head of Kachib presented to the Emir that his people wished to see him…he begged the Emir to go to Kachib. The Emir did and he and his group mostly mounted… among smooth rocks where horses were practically useless. They were set on by hundreds of Kaje pagans and seven of the Emir's people were killed while ten more were wounded. The Emir and his group scattered…thus attempted to make their way to Jema'a but were waylaid by Kaninkwons and five

---

[91]   Gaius Jatau, *The Colonial Economy*, p. 28.

[92]   Yusufu Turaki, *The British Colonial Legacy*, p. 91.

[93]   NAK NAS PROF: "Quarterly Report Ended 31st March, 1913"; S. Abubakar. "The Established Caliphate: Sokoto, the Emirates and their Neighbours." Ikime, O. *Groundwork of Nigerian History*. Ibadan: (Heinemann Educational Books (Nigeria) Plc., 1999), pp. 457-458.

women and two youths were murdered in cold blood and carried away to Kaninkwon.[94]

In a normal response by the British government, reinforcement was requested from Ogba-Umaisha for a counter attack. This strategy yielded positive results among the Kaje leading to a complete resettlement of their community, but it was never close to the desired result in Ninkyob land. Here is a lamentation by a colonial officer to that effect:

> The Kaninkwon-Abidoko still remain obstinate and refused to surrender the headhunting murderers harbouring in these villages...I am suspicious about this as it is positively affirmed by eye-witnesses that one of these village heads was the ringleader in the episode and in digging up buried bodies.[95]

In another report, there is information confirming that it was not easy for the British even with their superpower status. The information reveals thus:

> The Kaninkwom-Abidoko remain a serious problem. This is a group of pagans in a much lower scale than the Kaje. The Kaje is gradually giving up Headhunting and at his worse he only took the heads of males and females alike and will dig up the buried dead to do this also. He is also not particular as to whether the head is that of Kaninkwom or an alien.[96]

There is no certainty about the identity of the persons killed and their buried bodies dug up, but it seems that they must be strangers because, within Nikyob traditional practices, it is highly unthinkable for them to unearth the bodies of their loved ones who are already buried. The logical conclusion is that this must have been their way of hitting hard at the Indirect Rule system. In other words, these must have been bodies of colonial collaborators. Again, the Nikyob people are described as being on a much lower scale than the Kaje. This is too derogatory but very understandable; any group that yielded to British oppression was considered civilized. This is true because, in colonial philosophy, the Fulanis were often regarded as being of superior stock and

---

[94]   NAK: NASPROF 691/1915, September Quarterly Report 1915, by J.C. Sciortino.

[95]   NAK: NASPROF 691/1915, September Quarterly Report, J.C. Sciortino.

[96]   NAK: NAS PROF NO.2089, June 1915, Kaje and Kaninkwom Rising against Emir of Jemaa, by J.C. Sciortino, p.14.

civilization. For the Nikyob people, submitting to oppression was not an option and could not be considered a higher civilization.

This rejection of colonial domination took different forms despite the cruel repression by the British who were not ready to allow any opposition to stand on their way. Nikyob people sometimes deployed spiritual means to warn these invading forces:

> The half of "G" Company which had been lent the Province in June to assist in quelling certain disturbances and having completed these duties left Wamba for Lokoja on 2nd September. On the way to Loko one private was drowned at the Arichia ford during a general stampede caused by the accidental disturbance of a swarm of bees. The body has not yet been recovered.[97]

As earlier mentioned, nature also (through the factor of geography) made this area difficult for the British to overrun. Therefore, in addition to the advantage of their physical environment, spiritual power, and technology of using poisoned arrows were of great assistance; here is how the British described the physical environment:

> This village group is situated in very broken hilly country and the various quarters of the villages are hidden in deep ravines and thick bush, the approach to which is most difficult. It is therefore considered wise to leave these people to themselves till force is again available... This group can be dealt with when the Kaninkwoms are taken in hand. The latter (Kaninkwons) are situated some $12^{1/2}$ miles west of Jema'a, while the former some 20 miles south-east of Jema'a Native Administration but wish to be left alone... the Aro group of the Ayu District are merely truculent and decline to be administered.[98]

The report above is specifically about two ethnic groups - Nikyob and Ayu. However, a careful interrogation will reveal that the toughest battles for the British were among the Nikyob people. Further evidence again indicates that this resistance was not built on hate for any group of people but rather, a

---

[97]   NAK: NAS PROF 691/1915, September Quarterly Report 1915 by J.C. Sciortinon.
[98]   NAK: NASPROF, December Quarterly Report 1915, by J.C. Sciortino.

strong desire to be independent and free from interference. Another method of resistance to colonial conquest was that of evading taxation. The community usually refused to turn in their taxes whenever they were due, not for lack of it but because they considered the system as illegality.[99] The usual response from the colonial government to this recalcitrant attitude from any community was a ruthless destruction of both lives and property to serve as a deterrent as well as to force compliance. For instance, when the Native Authority agent went for the taxes due, he was only allowed to return alive but not with any collection. But the British replied to this action with inhumanity:

> Kaninkwom has not hitherto been fully administered and in fact the District Head (Madaikin Jemaa) visiting Kaninkwom to collect taxes last year was driven away. The punishment meted out to Kaninkwom-Abidoko is also severe and I am now hoping to get in touch with them through the other group of Kaninkwom (near Chunje) who are more amenable to being administered.[100]

For a British officer to acknowledge that the punishment was severe, means that it was not a good sight to behold. This ugly trend was not only from the side of the British as Nikyob was not left out in retaliating in order to assert their freedom and liberty. In the process of trying to assert their independence, they also often embark on cruelties against the perceived collaborators of the exploitative colonial system. Below is a graphic example of such encounters by both sides:

> On Monday 26th July we left Togwoi at 5:30 a.m. and crossing the River Tachab by the suspension bridge (which took one hour and 30 minutes) we arrived at Kaninkwom-Abidoko. This village is situated, in scattered quarters, in very broken country along well-wooded sullies and steep hill tops and armed natives were seen gliding through the bush everywhere and attempts were made to get in touch with them without success. These people were responsible for the murder of seven refugees (five of them women) from the scene of the attack on the emir. These seven were killed

---

[99]   Gaius Jatau. *The Colonial Economy,* p. 49.
[100] NAK: NAS PROF NO.2089, June 1915. Kaje and Kaninkwom Rising Against Emir of Jemaa, by J.C. Sciortino, p. 14.

on the Togwoi-Jemaa road (distance about 16 miles) at
various places which were pointed out to me. Rusty blood-
stains were clearly defined and the trampled grass indicated
which way the bodies had been dragged. In each case I
followed these tracks to attempt to trace remains. In every
case these tracks ended abruptly in small area of trampled
bloodstained grass and it was clear the victims had been cut
up and carried away piecemeal.[101]

Whenever the topic of the Indirect Rule era comes up for discussion,
some analysts have often ended up in the error of saying that the Nikyob of
that era failed by handing over lands to strangers. This is ignorance, to say the
least, and a great desecration of their hectic struggles, to say the worst. No
society including the Nikyob accepted foreign domination without resistance.
But resisting the British was tantamount to daring the military might of Great
Britain, the world's superpower at that time. This was done anyway with almost
nothing in terms of weapons and giving no regard for the consequences. Here
is what followed as a punishment for the above crime:

I therefore decided to destroy Kaninkwom-Abidoko and
when this was commenced there were attacks made and
arrows loosed from close range fell among us. One soldier
was hit in the chest but was immediately treated by Capt.
Waters and the wound was not fatal though the arrow was
heavily poisoned. Several arrows picked up were of the all-
wood variety; others were iron tipped.[102]

Every attempt by the Nikyob to reject the imposition of minority rule
could not stop the important British policy of the period. It only dragged the
enmity between them and the invaders with dire consequences as can be seen
above in the forms of the destruction of settlements, properties, and lives in
the process. Another instructive issue to note is that most of these punitive
measures by the British pushed Nikyob people away from the immediate
surroundings of the present day Kafanchan. They started returning when it
became obvious to them that colonialism had come to stay. Most of these
settlements were burnt down and the inhabitants had to escape to new

---

[101] This report was compiled in 1915 by the Acting Resident of Nasarawa Province. NAK: NAS PROF,
December Quarterly Report 1915, by J.C. Sciortino, p.11.
[102] NAK: NASPROF, December Quarterly Report 1915, by J.C. Sciortino, pp.11-12.

(secured) sites. The result is that new settlers including the elements of the emirate took over their lands.[103]

i.   The Indirect Rule System

Having demonstrated that the British occupation of Nikyob land was not done in a single day nor with fanfare, however, the superiority of Great Britain prevailed in the long run. The philosophy of Indirect Rule was built on the British philosophy of grading people in hierarchical order, with the British at the top of the ladder. In our area of study, the implication was that the European communities were above all races; then the Fulani group was considered subordinate to them but higher than the natives. Therefore, the responsibility of holding these groups together administratively was given to the Fulani minority. This choice was not because they conquered these people but because the British held the opinion that they were "civilized" and had equally developed an advanced political system.[104]

The assumption by many people, based on British propaganda is that they believe that Indirect Rule was collaboration between the British and the Africans to preserve the African socio-cultural organization; but the reality shows that it was neither collaboration nor indirect administration.[105] Everything was done with the sole aim of advancing British economic interests. This made repression the trademark of the system. The Fulanis were only work tools in the hands of the British with no initiative of their own except for extortion, intimidation, looting, and everything inhuman.[106] For administrative convenience and to also achieve maximum exploitation, the British created Jama'a Emirate in 1911.[107] The emirate was reorganized into four administrative districts with each having a District Head answerable to the Emir at Jama'a Daroro who, by this time, he was responsible to the District Officer (D.O.) who was a British. The districts under Jama'a were Kaje, Ayu, Ninzam, and the Jema'a Emirate itself. This structure later transformed into

---

[103]   This has been argued using court proceedings initiated by Mr. Jacob Jatau under the section on Kafanchan.

[104]   See, Yusuf Turaki, *The British Colonial Legacy*

[105]   Bala J. Takaya and Sonni Gwanle Tyoden (eds.), *The Kaduna Mafia: A Study of the Rise, Development and Consolidation of Nigerian Power Elite*, (Jos: University Press Ltd., 1987), p. 26.

[106]   During a discussion with Professor Alkasum Abba in his residence at Hanwa G.R.A. Zaria (on 22-10-2022), he revealed that the Native Authority was a system designed by the British to be cruel irrespective of who was put in charge of a political unit.

[107]   NAK: NAS PROF. Quarterly Report Ended 31st March, 1913.

Jema'a Federation.[108] Of all four districts, Jema'a District was the largest and the most populous covering an area of 676 sq. miles which is about 1081.6km. Its population consisted of the Numana, Kaninkon, Gwandara, and Mada; Hausa, Fulani, Birom, and Attakar.[109]

Under this system, Nikyob was given a Village Head as the colonial agent for easy tax assessment. The choice was more often based on the Native Authority's preference for a man who will serve as a willing agent; there was never regard for the interest of the people but the interest of the minority Europeans and the Native Authority as collaborators. It was also done to destroy any string of unity that could lead to a united force against colonial domination. But no amount of plan could stop this group of people from resisting Indirect Rule and what it stood for; the mission (Western) educated members of society kept championing the cause of liberation to the point that the British saw the futility of keeping this project (Jema'a District) as a single unit instead of disbanding it to ensure peace. The rejection of this arrangement was not only done by Nikyob but other groups within the area also showed rejection of this oppressive structure. Therefore, to achieve the best result, cooperation became the strategy adopted. The general atmosphere from the beginning of the creation of this political structure was one of tension and suspicion between the Nikyob and the emirate up to when it was reformed. This was what led to the creation of Kaninkon District in 1990 with Mallam Bako Galadima as the first District Head to assuage the demand for freedom from the emirate's oppressive rule. It only ended up serving as a morale booster as the efforts for self-rule kept growing as the people were emboldened.[110]

ii.   Christian Missionary Activities

Nikyob people are by all standards, very traditional, conservative, strict, and disciplined. This means that accepting change easily was difficult. As a result, it took the Christian missionaries years of repeated evangelization to be able to win their converts among these people. It was in 1932 that Christianity gained acceptance through the work of Mallam Toro. The first fruit of this labor was Pastor Tete Burat on 8 May 1932. His growth was so remarkable that in 1936 he was ordained a pastor; this means that he was the first pastor

---

[108]   Abdullahi Oumar Musa Ashafa (Jnr),"An Unexplored State", pp. 70-71.
[109]   Abdullahi Oumar Musa Ashafa (Jnr), "An Unexplored State", pp. 76-77.
[110]   Bauta D. Motty, *Indigenous Christian*, p. 7; Brief History of Bakin Kogi (Kyung) Kaninkon, (n.d, unpublished), p.20.

in Nikyob Land.[111] This was followed by Mallam Makama-Mang Kagoro, Garba Shuri, and Iperi on 11th of June of the same year.[112] Other prominent early converts were Mallam Sawan, Mallam Garba, and Mallam Dodo.[113] These early converts faced unimaginable opposition from their kinsmen for throwing away their established traditions in favor of the foreign system. But their perseverance with visible transformations in their lives and socio-economic status were attractions to many who later joined the new fold.

Another remarkable thing was that these Nikyob Christians walked from their communities to Kagoro for Sunday services. This was the practice until a church was built at Kafanchan town and then later at Gharas for Nikyob converts.[114] With this foundation, many mission stations sprang up and today, the entire land is filled with 99.9% of Christians with different denominations.

Not only was Christianity firmly established in Nikyob land, but it also gave birth to people who took the gospel to other communities far from their immediate environment. For instance, part of the enduring legacies of the Christian missions was the introduction of Western education. Consistent with Christian missionary practices, western education and religion (Christianity) were presented together. Hence, schools sprang up close to the mission stations; the first primary school by the Sudan Interior Mission (SIM) was in 1946 at Gharas (Ungwar Fari) under the mentorship of Mallam Dembo Kagoro. The pioneer learners were Yohanna Sam, Baba Jatau Jyad, Sabo Morik, Ladan Tete, Bitrus Majidadi, Kaho Majidadi, Matami Bazhin and James Sam.[115] Both Christianity and Western education have contributed significantly to the transformation of the land and the people.

[111]   Tanko Tete, *A Life of Service*, p. 44; Yahaya Emmanuel Banang, "Kaninkon (Ninkyob) Society: Historical & Contemporary Perspectives", (n.d., unpublished).

[112]   Yahaya Emmanuel Banang, "Kaninkon (Ninkyob) Society: Historical & Contemporary Perspectives", (n.d., unpublished).

[113]   Brief History of Bakin Kogi (Kyung) Kaninkon, (n.d, unpublished), p.20.

[114]   Yahaya Emmanuel Banang, "Kaninkon (Ninkyob) Society…"

[115]   Yahaya Emmanuel Banang, "Kaninkon (Ninkyob) Society…"

SECTION THREE:
POST-COLONIAL PERIOD

CHAPTER FOUR:

ASSERTING SELF-IDENTITY WITHIN INDEPENDENT NIGERIA

It has been demonstrated that the British subjugation was not welcomed with fanfare by Nikyob people; rather it was resisted vigorously through many strategies (violent and non-violent). The results of these struggles were mostly some forms of concession and not total acceptance of the demands for complete detachment from the Fulani (emirate) influence. Of course, the British knew the impossibility of keeping the whole natives under subjugation but kept playing around with the idea because it served their imperial purpose and was also a way of honoring their pact with the caliphate. However, due to persistent protests and resistance to the continued domination of the natives by the British through the emirate system, the colonial office promised to unbundle the unfair political system whenever the ruler ceased to live. This opportunity came when the British were busy with the preparations to hand over power to Nigeria. The implication is that the proposed change was held down by the Northern Regional Government.[116]

The same opportunity presented itself again in 1999 when the emir of Jama'a, Isa Muhammadu died. It once again revived the agitation for the dissolution of the emirate which was purely a colonial creation. The Kaninkon Chiefdom as we have today was not the first choice by the Nikyob people. The demand was for a single chiefdom for the Jama'a indigenes of the same status as the Jama'a emirate for the Hausa/Fulani community.[117] However, the government failed to honor this agreement in 1999 similar to the one in 1959; the disappointment in this pushed the indigenous peoples into a peaceful

---

116   Brief History of Bakin Kogi (Kyung) Kaninkon, (n.d, unpublished), p.19, see, The Kaninkon Community, Ungwar Fari District, "The Kaninkon Community of Jama'a Emirate in Retrospective". 1st October, 1992.

117   Brief History of Bakin Kogi (Kyung) Kaninkon, (n.d, unpublished), p.20.

protest against this highhandedness by the government. Consequently, the situation degenerated and caused the Kafanchan riot in 1999.[118]

Lastly, Kaninkon Chiefdom was created officially in December 2000 by Alhaji Ahmed Mohammed Makarfi, the then-executive governor of Kaduna State. The installation and presentation of the staff of office to the paramount ruler HRH Tanko Tete were performed on 20 January 2001.[119] The districts at the beginning of the chiefdom were three - Ungwar Fari, Dangoma and Bakin Kogi. Within a short period, the number increased to eight in all and they all had appointed District Headsthus: Ungwar Fari (Gbed Dick Dembo), Bakin Kogi (Gbed Bako Galadima), Ungwar Baki (Gbed Williams B. Gimba). The others are Goska (Gbed Moses Barde), Dangoma (Alhaji Samaila Suleiman), Amere (Gbed Ladan S. Adamu), Ambam District (Gbed Hosea D. Dodo), and Gerti (Gbed Stephen Daniel).[120]

[118]   Godwin Danjuma Kwalbe, "A History of Kafanchan to 2000", (Unpublished M.A. Project, Nasarawa State University, Keffi, 2016).
[119]   Tanko Tete, A Life of Service, p. 266.
[120]   Tanko Tete, A Life of Service, pp. 271-272.

CHAPTER FIVE:

THE PLACE OF KAFANCHAN IN NIKYOB (KANINKON) HISTORY

History of Kafanchan Town and its Many Dimensions

A lot information exists in research papers, journal articles; university projects, and internet materials on the history of Kafanchan many of which are controversial and some lack in-depth analysis and objective interpretation of the data available. The reason is that the town has attained prominence in the political economy of the region and the state at large. For instance, before the Federal Capital Territory was moved from Lagos to Abuja, a committee was inaugurated to choose a suitable replacement for Lagos; Dr. Nnamdi Azikiwe who was a member of the committee suggested that it be cited at Kafanchan.[121] Therefore, with such a national premium on the town, it has generated many conflicting histories and claims.

Conversely, the evolution of modern Kafanchan town cannot be understood in isolation from the factors that propelled the amalgamation of the Northern and Southern Protectorates in 1914. This move was made by Lord Lugard in 1902 passionately urging the colonial office to end the separate treatment of the two territories. His major interest in this amalgamation project was purely economic. He had argued that if this proposal was accepted and implemented, it would go a long way in ending the unnecessary antagonistic economic policies being implemented at the time by the same

---

[121] Godwin Danjuma Kwalbe & Ubaka Cosmas Molokwu, "A History of Colonial Cosmopolitan Town of Kafanchan; 1926-1960", being a paper presented at 67th Conference/Congress of Historical Society of Nigeria (HSN) on 25th-28th October, 2022 at the Nigerian Army Resource Centre, FCT, Abuja, p.1; Toure Kazah-Toure, "The Political Economy of Ethnic Conflicts and Governance in Southern Kaduna, Nigeria: [De] Constructing a Contested Terrain" in *Africa Development, Vol.24, No.1/2, issn. 08503907*, 1999, p. 135. Accessed at https://www.Jstor.org/stable/24484540 on 16/08/2022.

colonial office[122] which was definitely to its disadvantage. For instance, the Southern Administration had successfully built a railway line from Jebba to Minna which was meant to ease the process of moving resources of the Lagos hinterland; its northern counterpart built the Minna-Baro railway line.[123] Seeing these as tendencies to generate unhealthy rivalry, Lugard forcefully pushed for the unification of all transportation and communication infrastructures that cut across the two territories. Also, with the expanding economy of the Southern Region, this unification was envisaged as a support for the Northern Region until it became self-sufficient and subsequently relieved the British interest from bearing the financial burdens of the North in the form of Imperial Grant-in-Aid which was estimated at £300,000 per annum. This was in addition to the subsidy advanced by the Southern Protectorate.[124]

Consequently, Lugard and some British technocrats were assigned the responsibility of unifying the two protectorates. This project received another boost when Lugard was appointed the new Governor of Northern Nigeria saddled with the responsibility of unification. Therefore, his immediate action was to merge those departments of government he thought were critical to the overall control and administration of the country: Survey, Railway, Judiciary, Treasury, Military, Post and Telegraph, and the Audit Department. It was with these milestones that Lugard successfully midwifed the new country called Nigeria on 1 January 1914 as a single entity.[125] From this background, the railway appears to be undeniably central to the British colonial interest (economy). Therefore, this provides insight into why it was one of the earliest infrastructures to be developed by the British and also a major department singled out for the unification of government administrative departments. Generally speaking, the railway was to ease the evacuation of Nigerian products to Britain and other European countries.[126] However, in the process of serving their economic interest, the British could not deny Africans the positive

---

[122] P. D. Kums "Politica Development and Statehood in Nigeria, 1914-1979", In *The Amalgamation and a Century of Nigerian Nationhood*, by Terhemba Wuam & Victor Egwemi (eds), (Lagos: Bahiti & Dalila Publishers, 2016), p. 9.

[123] P. D. Kums, "Politica Development and Statehood in Nigeria, 1914-1979", In *The Amalgamation and a Century of Nigerian Nationhood*, by Terhemba Wuam & Victor Egwemi (eds), (Lagos: Bahiti & Dalila Publishers, 2016), p. 10.

[124] P. D. Kums, "Politica Development and Statehood in Nigeria", p. 10.

[125] P. D. Kums, "Politica Development and Statehood in Nigeria", p. 11.

[126] G. Jatau, *The Colonial Economy of Jema'a*, (Zaria: Ahmadu Bello University Press Limited, 2018), p. 116.

fallouts of their policies. One of these is the emergence of a cosmopolitan town that still stands out as a beehive of intergroup cooperation among Nigerians of diverse ethnic backgrounds.

However, it should be noted that before the building and completion of the Railway station at this location, there was already in existence, an intermediate village by the name of Kafanchan.[127] But the cosmopolitan town that grew from 1926 originally as a railway labour construction camp.[128] Today, it is an enduring footprint of British enterprise in Nigeria and Africa in general, and the product of labor from the natives.

The Growth and Development of Kafanchan Town

Construction of Railways

Before 1926, the surrounding landscape was dotted with clusters of settlements/hamlets. But, by 1915, the situation was going to change permanently due to a survey that was carried out purposely for the extension of the northeast Railway from Benue Bridge. This route was to run through Doma, Keffi, and Yeskwa District then proceeds northwest towards Kaduna. Progressively, in 1919, a route running west from Keffi through Abuja to Minna junction was also surveyed with a line running from Benue Bridge to Lafia and skirting the western slope of the Mada Hills, Jagindi, Bakin-Kogi, and Faddan Kagoro; then finally to Manchok (Moroa), Jos and Bukuru.[129]

However, the actual construction of the eastern line commenced in 1913 from Port Harcourt and reached the coalfields of Enugu in 1916, and Makurdi in 1924;[130] then finally, Kafanchan Junction was completed in 1926.[131] The choice of the area (Kafanchan) for a railway station was due to certain advantages it enjoyed; good flat and open land[132] and abundant economic opportunities which were of strategic interest to the colonial authority. Human labor was

---

[127]   NAK: Quaterly Report No. 61 for quarter ending 30th September, 1913; Godwin Danjuma Kwalbe, "The Evolution and Development of Kafanchan; 1927-1960", B.A. Project, A.B.U. Zaria, 2006, p.51.

[128]   NAK: PLA PROF 61/1928 "Report No. 41 for the year ending 31st December, 1927", by Colin R. Water.

[129]   A. H. M. Kirk-Greene, *Gazetteer of the Northern Provinces of Nigeria, Vol. III: The Central Kingdoms,* (London: Frank Cass & Company Ltd., 1972), p. 23.

[130]   A. L. Mabogunje, *Urbanisation in Nigeria,* (London: University Press Ltd., 1968), pp.144-145.

[131]   F. Jaekel, *The History of the Nigerian Railway, Vol.2,* (Ibadan: Spectrum Books Ltd., 1997), p. 190.

[132]   F. Jaekel, *The History of the Nigerian Railway,* pp. 190 & 205.

available and strategic, in addition to sufficient food and cash crops (millet, corn, ginger, pepper, and livestock) and mineral deposits such as limestone, tin, and columbite. The last mineral was scarce and global supply depended on Nigeria for the main ore of Niobium used in gas turbines, jet engines, and rockets. The implication of this is that Kafanchan Station became one of the most important stations in Nigeria.[133]

Town Planning

From this, one can infer that the choice of the site for a railway junction was governed by the British colonial interest of the day and not a desire to develop a town. The town, however, evolved in response to the activities engendered by this colonial interest. For instance, the effect of the extension of a railway from Kafanchan to Jos was dramatic; while it used to take 35 days for £29.10S for a ton of tin to be transported from Jos to the coast, subsequently, not only was the journey reduced to 35 hours, the cost came down to £8 per ton. At the same time, the amount of export increased from 10, 926 tons in 1927 to 13, 069 in 1928.[134]

The building of the railway station was done alongside the construction of European quarters for railway staff who would take charge of the various departments at this junction. Because of this, there also emerged temporary shelters by natives, Yoruba traders, contractors, laborers,[135] etc. who were attracted by the booming economic opportunities provided by this innovation in the transportation sector. Apart from the Igbo, Yoruba, and other ethnic groups that were not indigenous to the Southern Kaduna Zone, some of the natives also left their places to participate in the emerging capitalist economy. Following this development, one resultant effect of this process of urbanization was the loss of lands by the natives. This is revealed in the statement below:

> I wish to submit for your consideration the question of
> compensation to the native farmers owning the land in the
> vicinity of Kafanchan Junction, which is being acquired
> by Government for the proposed lay-out. This land is in
> part occupied by the natives who have settled in the old

---

[133]   F. Jaekel, *The History of the Nigerian Railway,* pp. 189-190.
[134]   A. L. Mabogunje, *Urbanisation in Nigeria,* pp. 145-146.
[135]   NAK: PLA PROF NO. 511/1926.

construction camp at Kafanchan. These natives have no
right whatsoever to the land on which they are squatting.[136]

There is no document presently to ascertain if this payment was made
and the identity of the recipients; however, it is enough evidence to discredit
the argument by Salisu Bala that Kafanchan was a Hausa-Fulani village and
the same as old Jama'a.[137] This argument is not tenable because the colonialists
never referred to the Hausa-Fulani Muslim group as natives. They were simply
referred to as Fulani, Hausa, or Mohammedans.[138] Strictly speaking, this new
town started as a construction camp that usually would have been destroyed
by the Construction Authority as soon as they did not need it but was left
to grow into a squatting community. This made the population surge rapidly
beyond the expectation of the colonial authority. The authority responded
by acquiring land from the natives to meet the need for expansion and to
start a community that was safe by all hygienic standards. These lands that
the authority acquired were recommended for compensation by the Colonial
Government at the cost of £3 per acre.[139]

Amid the growing population, the colonial authority had to produce a new
layout in 1928 with the survey plan numbered No. A6413 from the previous
plan M.287 that was prepared in July 1924.[140] This plan made provision for a
motorable way from the residential plot, six business plots, and a railway postal
agency. There was a provision within this new layout, for main roads of up to
18" wide and subsidiary roads of 12" wide. In all, the layout made provision
for social amenities right from the beginning of the new town.[141] This made
Kafanchan Town one of the few colonial settlements in Nigeria that were given
adequate attention with consideration for safety and future development.[142]
This desire to have a clean and safe town was demonstrated by the intention
to destroy the grass town that was springing up. Consequently, the authority
introduced the condition of registering plot holders as a strategy to drive
away the shanty type of buildings by persons described as "undesirables" who

---

[136]   NAK: PLA PROF NO. 662/1927; "Lay-out of Kafanchan", 28th September, 1927.
[137]   See , Salisu Bala, "The Foundation of Kafanchan, c. 1933: The Historical Background", in *Lapai Journal of Central Nigeria History, Vol. 2 Number* , March 2008, pp. 119-126.
[138]   Bala J. Takaya and Sonni Gwanle Tyoden (eds.), *The Kaduna Mafia, p. 51.*
[139]   NAK: PLA PROF: No.511/1926/29: " Kafanchan Lay-out", 19th October, 1927.
[140]   C.W. Rowling, *Report on Land Tenure: Plateau Province*, Kaduna, 1949, pp.43-44.
[141]   James Kantiyok, "The Establishment and Development of Kafanchan Town; 1927-1957", Unpublished B.A. Project, A.B.U. Zaria, p. 19.
[142]   NAK: PLA PROF NO.105/28/1 "Report for Quarter ended 30/9/1928", p.7.

were being attracted to the emerging settlement.[143] This was followed by the visit of the Senior Health Officer of the Northern Province in 1931 to ensure compliance with the outlined standards.[144]

Commercial Activities

With these huge economic potentials noticed early at this settlement, the African and Eastern Trading Association applied to have a trading site in 1927; the Niger Company was granted a holding right to a temporary site on the 1st of September while their agent arrived in Kafanchan on the 22nd September 1928 intending to clear the site and erect a building.[145] Subsequently, a market was established in 1930, but with an increase in population and commercial activities, it was relocated to a new site in 1950. The Native Authority augmented by building permanent stores and latrines in 1954.[146] It should be noted that the post office (established in 1928) served dual purposes of delivery of mail/parcels and financial transactions. This remained so because there was no bank then.

Administration and Security

To ensure the security of lives and property, Kafanchan town received its first police detachment of three constables in 1929.[147] Their activities were first restricted to the railway station and its immediate surroundings which had a great concentration of settlers. Then by 1933, ten bodyguards (*Yan Doka*) of the Emir were reorganized into the Native Authority Police Force which was used to police the entire town. However, due to the overwhelming responsibility before them, the District Officer (D.O.) had to write to the Provincial Resident, E.S. Pembleton at Jos in 1935 requesting for government police that should be stationed in the town to complement the efforts of the Native Authority Police Force. The Emir of Jama'a Mallam Muhammadu, on his part, requested the employment of six-night guards due to the rise in crime rates. In response to this request, a sub-detachment of 20 constables was established under a

---

[143]   NAK: PLA PROF NO.105/28/1 "Report for Quarter ended 30/9/1928", pp.7-8.
[144]   S. Sankey, "An Economic Geographical Survey of Kafanchan-Kaduna State", B.A. Geography, ABU, Zaria, 1983, pp.5-6.
[145]   NAK: PLA PROF NO.105/28/1 "Report for Quarter ended 30/9/1928", p.5.
[146]   James Kantiyok, "The Establishment of Kafanchan", p. 64-75.
[147]   James Kantiyok, "The Establishment of Kafanchan", p.39.

non-commissioned officer. In the same year, the Native Authority Prison was built and it commenced operation with about 33 prisoners having sentences ranging from 14 days to 1 year. Any sentence above 1 year was made only in Jos.[148]

Social Amenities

The matter of health care was given priority through sanitation. The sanitary officers embarked on house-to-house inspections and the defaulters were fined. A team of medical officers arrived in 1928 from Jos to inspect Kafanchan and eventually gave approval to a site close to the railway station for the construction of a hospital. This is the cradle of the present General Hospital now christened Sir Patrick Ibrahim Yakowa Memorial General Hospital, Kafanchan. It started as a health facility for railway workers but has since grown into a major medical referral center in the whole of Southern Kaduna. Due to its growing popularity and acceptance among the natives right from the beginning, the facility became inadequate leading to an extension that was completed in 1954 with additional specialized units like the X-Ray Section. This happened alongside the ante-natal clinic adjudged to be very successful.[149]

Efforts aimed at providing clean, safe, and portable drinking water yielded positive results in 1930 when four public wells were constructed at strategic locations. By 1938, six additional public wells were constructed for the immediate surroundings; then the town was provided with pipe-borne water in 1948, especially in public places like hospitals, markets, police barracks, prisons, and the European quarters. It was in 1957 that the streets were finally able to have taps and then the public wells were closed down. The railway corporation started providing electricity in the town albeit, limited to their quarters, offices, and locomotive sheds; some individuals within the mission stations provided private generating plants.[150]

For proper coordination of this new political space, the British introduced the machinery of Native Administration within the Indirect Rule system. The Native Administration was composed of three arms - Native Authority, Native Courts, and Native Treasuries. The bulk of the administrative work

---

[148]   James Kantiyok, "The Establishment of Kafanchan", pp. 41-45.
[149]   NAK ZAPROF 13/2/1495 "Jema'a Division Annual Report 1955", p.2.
[150]   S. Sankey, "An Economic Geographica Survey", p. 8; James Kantiyok, "The Establishment of Kafanchan…", pp.61-63.

revolved around the Emir, District Officer, and Resident Officer in that ascending order.[151] Jagindi, located not far from Kafanchan Town became the Headquarters of the Jema'a Division while Kafanchan Town was made the seat of Jama'a Emirate and also Jama'a Native Authority in 1933 with the transfer of Jama'a Emirate from Jama'a-Sarari (Madakiya) to Kafanchan.[152] This singular colonial decision gave a boost to the socio-political status of Kafanchan Town.

Christian Missions and Education

Christianity and Western Education were two major forces used to increase the pace of modernization and intergroup interactions in this area, as these churches brought together different people from various ethnic, cultural, and regional backgrounds. Since the bulk of the ethnic groups within the study area were not Muslims but adherents of African Traditional Religion (A.T.R.), they were available for proselytization by the Christian Missionaries. The Lugardian Administration in principle encouraged the Christian Missions among them but discouraged such activities among the Muslims based on an agreement not to disrupt their existing social structure. The first Christian Mission Station to be established in the whole of Southern Kaduna was in 1910 at Kwoi by The Reverend F.E. Hein of the Sudan Interior Mission (S.I.M.). This was followed by the second station at Kurmin Musa by Reverend T. Allen in 1921 and later, Reverend T. Archibald opened a station at Kagoro. The consequence of having these Mission Stations around was that by the 1930s, Kafanchan Town had in existence about four Christian Missions operating under the auspices of Sudan Interior Mission, Roman Catholic Mission, Baptist Mission, and Church Missionary Society.[153] The population of Christians was further increased in terms of size and diversity.

In the area of educational provision, in the southern part of the country, the Christian Missionaries were given a free hand for proselytization and education and the consequence was that the majority of the population became educated and consequently a threat to the colonial government. This made the British not give education a priority in their policy formulation and implementation. This position in Northern Nigeria implies that education was

---

[151]   Yusufu Turaki, *The British Colonial legacy,* pp. 54-92.
[152]   S. J. Hogben & A. H. M. Kirk-Greene, *The Emirates of Northern Nigeria,* (London: Frank Cass, 1966), p.554.
[153]   Yusufu Turaki. *The British Colonial...*p.110.

left to the Christian Missions, especially among the "pagans" who were taught Western civilization. Over time, this led to the emergence of two separate educational programs pursued within the context of colonial Nigeria. The target was the children of chiefs, teacher training centers, and technical/clerical schools. In the non-Muslim areas, the interest of the colonial government was to regulate the content of the curriculum in order not to allow the natives to get too much.[154]

It was at Kagoro, a few kilometers away from Kafanchan that the first Western school was established in 1929 by the S.I.M. The primary objective was to equip the natives with adequate knowledge of the Word of God so that they can in turn be able to evangelize out to their communities. In 1930, the Native Elementary School was established in Kafanchan Town officially as a school for Muslim boys. This was the first Elementary School that was established in Southern Zaria.[155] Subsequently, the real efforts toward providing education in this area came from Christian Missionaries: the Roman Catholic Mission set up a school in 1936, the Church Missionary Society established in 1937, the Sudan Interior Mission came in 1946 and the Baptist Church opened a school in 1952.[156]

Decolonization and the Nationalist Influence in Kafanchan Town

In the decolonization process of Nigeria, Kafanchan Town also played a very significant role. On 4 June 1946, a delegation of National Council of Nigeria and the Cameroons (N.C.N.C.) arrived in the town and held a successful rally at the Chrurch Missionary Society (C.M.S.) school ground. There were over 4,000 people in attendance. At the end of the rally, a resolution was reached mandating the leadership of N.C.N.C. to represent the people of Kafanchan. Then railway workers on their part organized a special ceremony to honor Pa Michael Imoudu, the President of the Railway Workers Union for his sacrifices.[157]

---

[154]   Yusuf Turaki. *The British Colonial…* pp.76-87.

[155]   Yusuf Turaki, *The British Colonial Legacy,* pp. 113-119.

[156]   James Kantiyok, "The Establishment of Kafanchan", pp. 54-63.

[157]   Alkasum Abba, *The Northern Elements Progressive Union and the Politics of Radical Nationalism in Nigeria; 1938-1960.* (Zaria: The Abdullahi Smith Centre for Historical Research, 2007), p. 58.

With the inception of the Macpherson Constitution in January 1950,[158] the Northern People's Congress (N.P.C.) emerged as the anointed party of the Native Authority (N.A.) in the north. This did not stop the existence of other political organizations instead their existence became a threat to the northern Emirs and Chiefs, and to some extent an enmity with the British establishment. The presence and activities of the radical Northern Elements Progressive Union (N.E.P.U.) were felt among the inhabitants of this town.[159] Nevertheless, because the Native Authority Administration was sustained by segregation and oppression of the natives who were considered labor reserves and tax contributors to the colonial economy. Many of them during the decolonization period were involved with such political organizations as the Action Group (AG) and United Middle Belt Congress (U.M.B.C.).[160] To the NPC-led government in northern Nigeria, this step was considered an affront to the northern establishment; while to the former, it was a deliberate action to weaken and break the stranglehold of the Caliphate on a people that were never conquered during the Sokoto Jihad.[161] This opposition to minority rule continued throughout colonial domination.

Kafanchan; A Place or an Ethnic Group?

Studying the history of Kafanchan Town so far allows one the opportunity to appreciate its history especially, the obvious cultural diversity and unity. In pre-colonial times, the area was a whole zone of fruitful intergroup cooperation among various indigenous groups. There were no rigid boundaries among these unique and culturally similar ethnic groups. Their identity remained as such until the eighteenth century when the demographics started changing with the migration of Fulani pastoralists, Hausa traders, and slave raiders in direct response to abundant economic opportunities and the presence of the Trans-Saharan trade route that passed through this area to Keffi and the entire Benue Valley.[162] During colonial times, the name Kafanchan featured

---

[158]   Alkasum Abba, *Contemporary Nigerian Politics and the Ghost of the Politics of the Independence Struggle*, (Zaria: Ahmadu Bello University Press Limited, 2022), p.16.

[159]   In a private discussion with my father Mr. Danjuma Gaga Kwalbe shortly before he died, he told me that his own father (my grandfather), Mr. Kwalbe Mere was an active NEPU politician under Jama'a Native Authority.

[160]   Yusufu Turaki. *British Colonial Legacy*, pp. 224-226.

[161]   Matthew Hassan Kukah, *Religion, Politics and Power in Northern Nigeria*, (Ibadan: Spectrum Books Ltd., 1993), pp. 7 & 8.

[162]   Simon Yohanna, *The National Question: Ethnic Minorities and Conflicts in Northern Nigeria*, (Kagoro: Mikrom Prints, 2008), pp. 146-147.

as a village and the greater part of it was inhabited by the Kaninkon ethnic group[163]; but its borders were transitional precincts among the indigenous groups within the area of studies such as the Kagoro and Kaje.

It was not a name of an ethnic group but a village. The evidence from tax assessment records which were based on "tribal" units does not reveal Kafanchan as one (ethnic group). This cannot be disputed because the British colonial economy survived on taxation and could not have ignored such a "tribe" assuming it was in existence in such an open area. The tax assessment was done based on ethnic groups using various village and community heads for effective collection and enforcement. Moreover, a compilation by Greenberg which was later edited by Abdullahi Smith has no tribal group as Kafanchan.[164] However, the process of urbanization attracted many natives which led to the fusion of similar languages over time, and ultimately a separate language group emerged and adopted the name Kafanchan. This is seen with the later appearance of the name Kafanchan as an ethnic group on the colonial tax assessment record that had a population of less than a thousand people in 1935.[165]

Kafanchan in Nikyob History

As stated earlier, before 1926 when the railway station was completed at its present site in our area of study, there was a village by the name of Kafanchan associated with the Nikyob people. This is verifiable within the available historical data below, in addition to the above presentation. When giving an account concerning the difficulty the colonizers had in administering the natives, a murder case is said to have occurred at a:

---

[163] There was a long running legal battle in 1973-1974 between Mr. Jacob Jatau (Appellant) a Kaninkon man and Alhaji Isa Mohammed (Respondent), the then Emir of Jama'a; it was over farm land seized by the father of Isa Mohammed when the British relocated the emirate from Madakiya to Kafanchan in 1933. This case began at Kafanchan Area Court to Upper Area Court Zaria and ended at The High Court of Justice, Kaduna. The final judgement was unfairly in favour of the respondent for obvious reasons.

[164] Abdullahi Smith, *A Little New Light,* (Zaria: Abdullahi Smith Centre for Historical Research. 1987), pp.18-21; C.L. Temple, *Tribes, Provinces, Emirates and States of the Northern Province of Nigeria,* (London: Frank Cass, 1965).

[165] Provincial Gazetteer. 2088/1918."Jama'a Divisional Affairs". Additionally, the latest available list of Nigerian languages by Keir Hansford, John Bendor-Samuel, and K. Standford, updated in May 2004 by the more recent research work of scholars, including, D. Crozier, R. Connell and U. Siebert, published in *Ethnologue: Languages of the World,* 14th Edition identifies 505 living languages in Nigeria. This is an increase by 111 from the 394 living languages identified in 1976, see Yusufu Bala Usman & Alkasum Abba, *The Misrepresentation of Nigeria,* pp. 38, 93-98.

> Village called Kafanchan where two men were reported to
> have been killed. The village refused to come in to Jema'a
> when called, and opposed a small party of 20 men who
> under Lt. Garnier accompanied Mr. Migeod. There were
> only 2 casualties amongst the villagers none on our side. The
> difficulty has been overcome, and the headmen concerned
> have promised to try and capture the murderers.[166]

This establishes the fact that a settlement existed in this area with the
name Kafanchan and was inhabited by the natives. Furthermore, the same
officer in another report in the area provided some positive reports about the
Emir of Jema'a taking his duties seriously:

> He has twice visited outlining districts in the past quarter,
> once to Kafanchan to witness the execution of four
> headhunters, and again to investigate a matter or refusal to
> obey orders by Village Head in the Kaje District.[167]

This execution above was carried out in the village of the culprits to make
it a public warning against the community for always indulging in such acts.
Their identity (ethnicity) was revealed in another report:

> I regret to record there is still reason to believe that the
> deplorable practice of "head hunting" has not yet been finally
> stamped out. Early in the quarter two Jemaa boys were sent
> by their father to collect ashes at Kaninkwom. As they did
> not return, enquiries were made and it was ascertained that
> the boys never arrived at their destination. Marks of a recent
> struggle were seen in the bush close to the road these boys
> took and local opinion has it that they were murdered. I was
> on tour at the time but I understand the Resident instructed
> the Emir to make a searching enquiry into this matter. So
> far, however, the Emir's efforts have proved fruitless and
> there seems but little chances of finding out what really
> occurred.[168]

---

[166]   NAK NAS PROF 3763/1911. "Quarterly, Half-Yearly and Annual Reports", by Major H.D. Larry
More.
[167]   NAK NAS PROF 1913/1. "Annual Report 1913", by H.D. Larry More.
[168]   NAK NAS PROF 94/1915. "Second Quarterly Report 1914", by J.C. Sciortino.

The punishment for the murder of the Jemaa boys as captured above was done in the community where they lived, that is Kafanchan. It was on purpose and in 1913. This is logical since the immediate quotation was from a 1914 report which shows that it was a reflection. If the punishment was in the village where the culprits lived and the boys went to collect ashes at Kaninkwom village, the picture is clear as to who inhabited Kafanchan village.

Furthermore, when the Emir and his men were ambushed, the party scattered in different directions looking for safe locations. In the process, some of them made their way into the Nikyob settlement. The report of this skirmish provides us with evidence in support of our argument:

> ...some of the Emir's people had made for Jemaa and while crossing the Bakin Kogi ford the Bakin Kogi people (a village about ¼ mile from Togwoi) came out and killed some of them. Mallam Sambo father of Mallam Sharubutu was killed at Bakin Kogi by Bakin Kogi people with an arrow. His women scattered and some were found in the bush by pagans of Kaje and others by **pagans of Kaninkwom of Kaffanchan** and guided safely to Jemaa. Others who took the direct road after escaping Bakin Kogi's attack were waylaid by Kaninkwom of Abidoko and murdered on the road and carried away.[169]

The highlighted line above is enough proof of the inhabitants of this village referred to as Kafanchan. This is further corroborated by an anthropological map of Plateau Province as compiled in 1920 by J.C. Sciortino. The map shows the entire expanse of land occupied by the Nikyob people in the early colonial period, within the Jema'a Division. However, it does not provide any clue about a group of people known as Kafanchan. The entire surrounding is presented with names of groups that still occupy portions of the landscape.[170]

---

[169]   NAK ZAR PROF 2089. "Kaje and Kaninkon Uprising against Emir of Jemaa, 1915".
[170]   J.C. Sciortino, *Gazeteer of Northern Provinces of Nigeria; Vol. III* (London: Frank Cass & Co. Ltd, 1920) p.5.

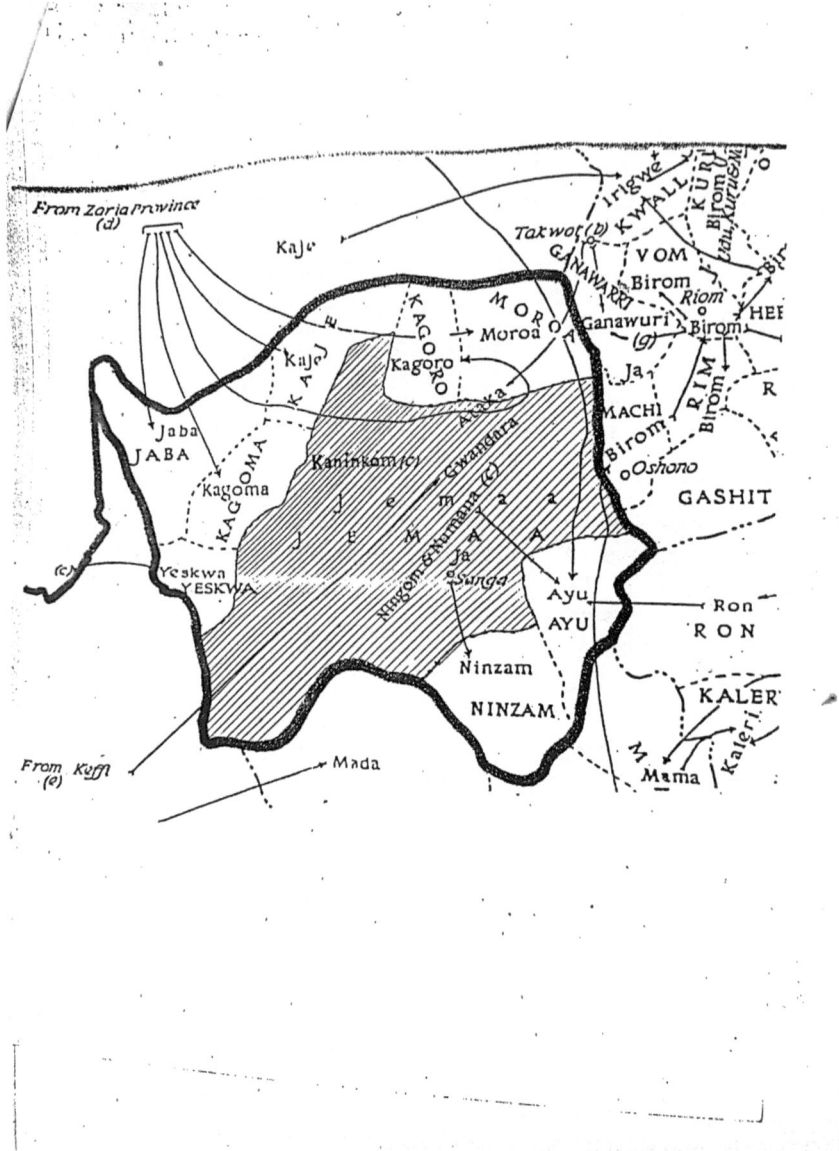

Plate 1: Colonial Map of the Area of study
Source: *Gazetteer of Northern Provinces of Nigeria Vol. III*

In a final analysis, a survey of Kafanchan Town in its modern state reveals names of streets alien to the entire Southern Kaduna area. This is not an accident of history but a normal process; the streets were named after the places of origin of those settled in the particular portion. Of course, it has earlier been demonstrated that the new town attracted many visitors who took up residence to benefit from the economic opportunities offered by the railway station. Therefore, in honor of the natives, one street was given the name Kaninkon.[171] This remains an enduring legacy of the relationship between the Kafanchan village and the Ninkyob people. Apart from the entrance in the northern part and exit in the southern part which is rightly named Kagoro Road and Ungwar Rimi Road respectively, there are no such names with a close connection to the Southern Kaduna groups.

---

[171]   No street in Kafanchan Town bears the name of any ethnic group around the environment.

CHAPTER SIX:

CONCLUSION

This is the history of the Nikyob people within the context of autochthonous groups in central Nigeria. Using the facts of history, this book has helped to lay to rest the longheld, but illogical and unscientific view of Ninkyob migration/ origins from Katsina-Ala, Kano, Bauchi, Taraba, etc. This is no longer tenable in the light of indisputable pieces of evidence (archaeological, cultural, and linguistic); the groups that the Nikyob people share some clear similarities with are their immediate neighbors. This suggests longtime interactions leading to cultural and linguistic exchanges. Moreover, the group was categorically marked "unknown" by European writers because they could not trace them beyond their present environment.

Again, the ability to relate with one's neighbors is a precondition for peaceful coexistence in an area. This, the Nikyob people have done for many years with their neighbors. There are also of evidence of robust intergroup relations between Nikyob and other groups around their environment. It is worthy of note that the factor of the environment holds a key to understanding the history of this group of people. With everything available for human survival, the choice of this settlement was based on its potential for agriculture and the huge mineral deposits. There was also a strategic (security) purpose for this choice as the area was full of mountain ranges, valleys, caves, woodlands, etc. that served as hideouts from invading armies.

With this, the area had remained their home for so long with only localized migrations to search for new fertile lands, and hunting grounds and also relocating from forceful subjugation by European occupiers. The landmass which was once occupied by this group in pre-colonial times has shrunk in size and this is due, in part, to the fact that boundaries were fluid and as a result of the constant punitive actions undertaken by the colonizers. In order to survive, they took the option of always relocating to safer grounds that were difficult to be traced by the invaders. Consequently, these vacant spaces were always taken over by the agents of the colonialists.

Generally, this group has contributed through hard labor and taxation to the building of modern Nigeria both during colonial rule and after independence. By this, it was incorporated into the world capitalist economy; so as to survive the new political economy, the Nikyob people adjusted by taking advantage of the forces of change that came with colonialism - Christianity and Western education. As a result, the group is now part and parcel of the modernization/globalization seeping across the world.

Interestingly, this historical study provides an opportunity for reflection and projection for the community as a whole and individuals in particular. This is possible after appreciating the various phases of transformation that the people have passed through. It is too late to reverse certain things back to their pre-colonial state but it is not too late to restrategize for the years ahead especially being armed now with the knowledge of history. Historical knowledge is the bedrock for the development and transformation of every human society and Nikyob is not an exception.

BIBLIOGRAPHY

A. PRIMARY SOURCES

i. ORAL INTERVIEW

1. Barde Mbom Biang, interviewed at U/Fari Kaninkon, Kafanchan (23/03/2006.

2. Tukura Kpat, interviewed at U/Fari Kaninkon, Kafanchan (23/03/2006).

3. Samuel Maigida, interviewed at U/Masara, Kafanchan (23/03/2006).

4. Abdullahi (*Sarkin Dawaki Jama'a*), interviewed at Borno Street, Kafanchan (25/03/2006).

5. Pastor (Barr.) Wakili Kadima, interviewed at Jos Street, Kafanchan (10/12/2012).

6. Tanko Tete, interviewed at Bakin-Kogi, Kaninkon, Kafanchan (27/07/2022).

7. Alhaji Waje Damina (Dangaladiman Dangoma), Interview, a retired army officer, 81 years old. 28-12-2016.

8. Alkasum Abba, interviewed in his residence at Hanwa G.R.A. Zaria (on 22-10-2022).

ii. ARCHIVAL SOURCES

NAK: Quarterly Report No. 61 for quarter ending 30th September, 1913.

NAK: PLA PROF. 61/1928, "Report No. 41 for the year ending 31st December, 1927", by Colin R. Water.

NAK: NAS PROF,"December Quarterly Report 1915".

NAK: PLA PROF NO. 662/1927; "Lay-out of Kafanchan", 28th September, 1927.

NAK: NAS PROF. "Quarterly Report Ended 31st March, 1913".

NAK: ZAR PROF. C. 28 Vol. II "Jama'a Division Affairs".

NAK: PLA PROF NO. 511/1926.

NAK: PLA PROF No.511/1926/29: "Kafanchan Lay-out", 19th October, 1927.

NAK: ZAPROF 13/2/1495 "Jema'a Division Annual Report 1955".

NAK: PLA PROF NO.105/28/1 "Report for Quarter ended 30/9/1928".

NAK: NAS PROF 3763/1911. "Quarterly, Half-Yearly and Annual Reports", by Major H.D. Larry More.

NAK: NAS PROF 1913/1. "Annual Report 1913", by H.D. Larry More.

NAK: NAS PROF 94/1915. "Second Quarterly Report 1914", by J.C. Sciortino.

NAK: ZAR PROF 2089. "Kaje and Kaninkon Uprising Against Emir of Jemaa, 1915".

NAK: SNP 3763/1911 "Nasarawa Province; Report for June Quarter, 1911".

NAK: NAS PROF 94P/1915 "Second Quarterly Report 1914".

NAK: NAS PROF 984/1915 " 'G' COMPANY, ON MADA PATROL", by J.C. Sciortino.

NAK: ZAR PROF 1770; "Tribal and Administrative organization Report", by A.B. Matthews.

NAK: NAS PROF. "Quarterly Report Ended 31st March, 1913".

B.   SECONDARY SOURCES

i.   PUBLISHED BOOKS

Abba, A. *The Northern Elements Progressive Union and the Politics of Radical Nationalism in Nigeria; 1938-1960*. Zaria: The Abdullahi Smith Centre for Historical Research, 2007.

-   *Contemporary Nigerian Politics and the Ghost of the Independence Struggle*. Zaria: Ahmadu Bello University Press Ltd., 2022.

Abubakar, S. "The Established Caliphate: Sokoto, The Emirates." In *Groundwork of Nigerian History*, by Obaro Ikime. Ibadan: Heinemann Educational Books (Nigeria) Plc., 1999.

Ames, C.G. *Gazetteers of the Northern Provinces of Nigeria, Volume III: The Central Kingdoms (Kontagora, Nasarawa, Nupe, Illorin).* London: Frank Cass, 1972.

Bala, S., and Sani Abubakar Lugga, *Jama'a Emirate: The Establishment and the Transformation of Jama'a Emirate in Northern Nigeria.* Katsina: Lugga Printing Press, 2021.

Buchanan, K.M. *Land and People in Nigeria.* London: University of London Press, 1955.

Hogben, S.J. & A.H.M. Kirk-Greene. *The Emirates of Northern Nigeria.* London: Frank Cass, 1966.

Ikime, O. *History, The Historian and The Nation: The Voice of a Nigerian Historian.* Ibadan: Heinemann Educational Books (Nigeria) PLC, 2006.

Jaekel, F. *The History of the Nigerian Railway.* Ibadan: Spectrum Books, 1997.

James, I. *Studies in the History, Politics and Cultures of Southern Kaduna Peoples Groups.* Jos: Ladsomas Press Limited, 1997.

Jatau, G. *The Colonial Economy of Jema'a; 1900-1960.* Zaria: Ahmadu Bello University, 2018.

Kaninkon Chiefdom. *The Pioneers.* (n.d.), Hill-Side Production.

Kirk-Greene, A.H.M. *Gazetteer of the Northern Provinces, Vol. III: The Central Kingdoms.* London: Frank Cass, 1972.

Kukah, M.H. *Religion, Politics, and Power in Northern Nigeria.* Ibadan: Spectrum Books Ltd., 1993.

Kums, P. D. "Politica Development and Statehood in Nigeria, 1914-1979." In *The Amalgamation and a Century of Nigerian Nationhood*, by Terhemba Wuam & Victor Egwemi (eds). Lagos: Bahiti & Dalila Publishers, 2016.

Kunhiyop, S.W., *African Christian Theology.* Nairobi: HippoBooks, 2012.

Mabogunje, A.L. *Urbanisation in Nigeria.* London: University Press, 1968.

Smith, A. *A Little New Light.* Zaria: Abdullahi Smith Centre for Historical Research, 1987.

Smith, M.G. *Government in Zazzau.* Oxford University Press, 1960.

Takaya, B. J. and Sonni Gwanle Tyoden (eds). *The Kaduna Mafia: A Study of The Rise, Development and Consolidation of a Nigerian Power Elite*. Jos: University Press Ltd, 1987.

Tete, T. *A Life of Service: Autobiography of Sarkin Kaninkon (Tum Ninkyob)*. Makurdi: Aboki Publishers, 2020.

Temple. *Tribes, Provinces, Emirates and States of the Northern Province of Nigeria*. London: Frank Cass, 1965.

Turaki, Y. *The British Colonial Legacy in Northern Nigeria: A Social Ethical Analysis of the Colonial and Post-Colonial Society and Politics in Nigeria*. Jos: ECWA Productions Ltd., 2017.

-    *The Trinity of Sin*. Nairobi: HippoBooks, 2011.

Yohanna, S. *The National Question: Ethnic Minorities and Conflicts in Northern Nigeria*. Kagoro: Mikrom Prints, 2008.

ii.   JOURNALS

Bala, Salisu. "The Foundation of Kafanchan, c.1933: The Historical Background." *Lapai Journal of Central Nigeria History*, 2008.

Fagg, B.E.B. "The Nok Culture in Pre-History." *Journal of Historical Society of Nigeria, Vol.1, No.1*, 1957.

Gbadamosi, T.G.O. & J.F.Ade Ajayi. "Islam and Christianity in Nigeria", in Ikime, Obaro. *Groundwork of Nigerian History*. Ibadan: Heinamann Education Books (Nigeria) Plc., 1999.

Grebe, K. and Wilfred Fon, *African Traditional Religion and Christian Counselling*. India: Oasis International Limited, 2007.

Kwalbe, G.D., "Intergroup Relations in Jama'a Division; 100-1987", in *Kaduna Journal of Humanities, Volume 6, Number 1, 2022, ISSN: 2636-6436*. Kaduna: Department of History, Kaduna State University.

Kwalbe, G.D., Mikah Nuhu Adamu & Sulaiman I. Richifa. "An Appraisal of the African World View and Orthodox Medicine within Kafanchan Town, Kaduna State", in *POLAC International Journal of Economics and Management Science (PIJEMS), Vol.8, No.1, April 2022, ISSN: 2465-7085*. Department of Economics and Management Science Nigeria Police Academy, Kano.

C.   INTERNET SOURCE

Kazah-Toure, T. "The Political Economy of Ethnic Conflicts and Governance in Southern Kaduna, Nigeria: [De] Constructing a Contested Terrain." *African Development, Vol. 24, No. 1/2, Issn. 08503907,* 1999: 104-144; accessed at https://www.Jstor.org/stable/24484540 on 16/08/2022.

Kaduna Mining Development Co. LTD. (KDMC). "Mineral Endowments" https://kmdc.kdsg.gov.ng/mineral-endowments/ (31-08-2022).

Olumbe,D. "African Worldview: An introduction", July 2008. Retrieved from https:///watumishiwaneno.files.wordpress.com/2014/08/African_worlview_introduction.pdf (21-09-2021).

Roscoe Stanyon, Marco Sazzini & Donata Luiselli. "Timing the First Migration into Eastern Asia" in *Journal of Biology, ISSN: 1475-4924,* 2009. Accessed at https://doi.org/10.1186/jbiol115 (22/08/2022).

D.   PROJECTS/THESES, PAPERS AND MEMORANDA

Abdul, H.A. "Pre-Colonial History of Nindem and their Neighbours in Godogodo Chiefdom, Kaduna State, Up to 1904". Unpublished M.A. Project (History), KASU, 2018.

Adon, A. "Kaningkon and Their Neighbours". Unpublished manuscript, (n.d.).

Ashafa (Jnr,) A.O.M. "An Unexplored State of the Sokoto Caliphate in Southern Zaria: A History of the Jema'a Emirate; C.1800-1967". (Unpublished B.A. Project, Bayero University, Kano, 1991).

Banang, Y.E. "Kaninkon (Ninkyob) Society: Historical & Contemporary Perspectives". (n.d., Unpublished Manuscript).

Civil Record of Appeal. Upper Area Court Zaria. Appeal No. NCH/33A/74. (28/6/1974).

Indigenous Peoples Forum, Kafanchan. "Memorandum on the Undercurrent that gave Expression to the Crisis from the Perspective of an Active Participant in the Negotiations for a Peaceful Resolution of the Issue of Self-Determination in Kafanchan Area (Jema'a)". 10th June, 1999.

Indigenous Peoples Forum, Kafanchan. "Kafanchan Crisis: The Peace Issue in Jema'a Emirate (Kaduna State)". 24th June, 1999.

Kafanchan Area Court No.2. (16/7/1973) .

Jatau, J. "Taka itace Tahirin Kaninkon". Unpublished manuscript, (n.d.); Ayuba Adon. "Kaningkon and Their Neighbours". Unpublished manuscript, (n.d.).

Jatau, J. "Baiyyani A Kan Sarautan Ungwan/Baki". 18th May, 1978.

Kaninkon Development Association (KADA). "Memorandum to the Judicial Panel of Enquiry into the Kafanchan Crisis of May 22nd, 1999: The Position of the Kaninkon Community".

Kaninkon Development Association (KADA). "Memorandum to the Judicial Panel of Enquiry into the Kafanchan Crisis of May 22nd, 1999: The Position of the Kaninkon Community".

Kantiyok, J. "The Establishment and Development of Kafanchan Town; 1927-1957", Unpublished B.A. Project, A.B.U. Zaria.

Kwalbe, G.D. "The Evolution and Development of Kafanchan; 1927-1960." Unpublished B.A. Project (History) A.B.U. Zaria, 2006.

Kwalbe, G.D. "A History of Kafanchan to 2000". Unpublished M.A. Project (History), NSUK, 2016.

Kwalbe, G.D & Ubaka Cosmas Molokwu. "A History of Colonial Cosmopolitan Town of Kafanchan; 1926-1960", a paper presented at 67th Conference/Congress of Historical Society of Nigeria (HSN) on 25th-28th October, 2022 at the Nigerian Army Resource Centre, FCT, Abuja.

Kwalbe, G.D. "Re-Southern Kaduna Muslim Ummah Development Association (SOKAMUDA): Letter of advice on recurring communal Disturbances in Southern Kaduna Particularly recent ones in Kajuru, Zangon-Kataf and Kajuru Local Government Areas of Kaduna State." 16th July 2020.

Kwalbe, G.D. "Re: Hausa/Fulani Community Lays Claim to Southern Kaduna". 18th August, 2020.

Moses, M. "Levels and Differentials in Fertility at Kafanchan." Unpublished M.A. Project (Geography) A.B.U. Zaria, 1985.

Sankey, S. "An Economic Geographical Survey of Kafanchan-Kaduna State." Unpublished B.A. Project (Geograph) A.B.U. Zaria, 1983.

The Kanignkom Community, Ungwar Fari District. "The Kaningkom Community of Jema'a Emirate in Retrospective". 1st October, 1992.

The History Project. "Brief History of Bakin Kogi (Kyung) Kaninkon" (n.d).

The Kaninkon Community, Ungwar Fari District. "The Kaninkon Community of Jama'a Emirate in Retrospective". 1st October, 1992.

Yohanna, S. "Southern Zaria in Historical Perspectives", A Paper Presented in Room 79, F.A.S.S. Building, A.B.U Zaria, 1982.

ABOUT THE AUTHOR

Godwin Danjuma Kwalbe is currently running two Ph.D. programs at the Department of History and Diplomatic Studies, University of Abuja, and the Department of Christian Theology of Public Policies, ECWA Theological Seminary, Kagoro, respectively. He holds a Master of Arts Degree in History from Nasarawa State University, a Diploma in Innovation and Entrepreneurial Finance from Kaduna Business School, a Professional Diploma in Education (PDE), and a B.A. (Hons.) History from Ahmadu Bello University, Zaria. His research interest includes Political History, Public Policies, Inter-Group Relations, Minority, and Religious Issues among others.

He previously taught at Peace Science International School, Anglican Junior Seminary, and Mercy Incubator Schools all at Kafanchan; this was before working as a full-time pastor for six years with Operation Catch-The-Fire Ministry where he served as the Resident Pastor of the Main Church at No. 17, Abuja Street, Kafanchan. From there, he joined the Faculty at the Department of History, Kaduna State University as a tenured staff. He has been involved in teaching and research at the same institutions with various papers published in different journals, both local and international.

A History of The Nikyob (Kaninkon) People, c.1750-2000 is his first book to be published; there are other manuscripts ready for publication anytime soon. Presently, he lives in Kaduna with his wife Grace, and their three children - Teb-Rik, Veh-Tum, and Nnyok-Rik.